SMALL GROUP

H E L P

GUIDES

I'm a now what?

by
Michael Mack

Standard PUBLISHING

I'm A Leader...Now What?
Published by Standard Publishing,
Cincinnati, Ohio

www.standardpub.com

Produced by Susan Lingo Books™

14 13 12 11 10 09 08 07   9 8 7 6 5 4 3 2 1
978-0-7847-2076-9

DEDICATION

This book is dedicated to the best small group leader ever. Many thanks to all the small group leaders and members who have had an impact on my life and this book.
Thanks to those whose help made this book happen: Heidi, Larry, Katie, Diedre, Mark, Jennifer, Cheryl, and Susan.

Contents

The Best Small Group Leader Ever

I'M A SMALL GROUP LEADER...
NOW WHAT?

I think that's a good question—one that lots of small group leaders ask at one time or another. And you don't need to be a new leader to ask the question. Even veterans need to ask, *Now what?* every once in a while.

I came across this Top Ten List on the SmallGroups. com web site: "Top Ten Things They Forgot to Mention During Your Small Group Leader Training." One of my favorites on the list was, "Enjoy the journey...You are now on your own!"

That's probably how many small group leaders feel, but I have good news! No, you're not going to save a lot of money on your car insurance. But as a small group leader you are not alone. These Small Group HELP! Guides from Standard Publishing walk with you through all of the issues and challenges of leading a group. But that's still not the best news! Here it is: you have the best small group leader ever available to help you lead your group. Wow. That *is* good news!

I've written this book not because I'm the best small group leader ever—I'm not—but to help you learn from and thus become more like the best small group leader ever: Jesus! I'll discuss six things Jesus did as he led his small group for three years, and I'll apply what I've learned to helping you lead your small group:

✔ **Seek** – Jesus' leadership began with his personal relationship with his heavenly father. So should ours.

✔ **Surrender** – Jesus yielded his heart and ministry to God. So should we.

✔ **Shepherd** – Jesus was known as the Good Shepherd and he is our Chief Shepherd. We, too, are called to shepherd, as his subordinates.

✔ **Serve** – Jesus came as a servant...to his group and to the world. That's our calling as leaders as well.

✔ **Share** – Jesus shared the load and built a team...a team that could continue after he "moved on." What can we learn from him about sharing leadership?

✔ **Steward** – Jesus looked at his ministry as a matter of stewardship. We can learn a lot from his view-point of leadership.

WHAT IS A SMALL GROUP LEADER?

Let's make sure we're on the same page right from the beginning. Throughout this book I'll continue to define what a small group leader is, but perhaps it will help to start by looking at some potential small group leaders to show what a small group leader is not.

C a u t i o n

This is not a book about the skills needed to facilitate a small group meeting. This book deals more with the internal qualities that make a good leader. My aim is to help you become a leader after God's own heart (1 Samuel 13:14).

Hannah Hostess

A small group leader is more than a host or hostess who opens up his or her home to the group. While this is a very worthy role in the group, the leader has a different assignment.

Ferdinand Facilitator

Hannah and Ferdinand are related. A small group leader is more than just a discussion facilitator. This may be part of the role of a leader, but only a small part.

Billy Bible Scholar

Billy might be a good small group leader, but not based on his superior knowledge of the Bible or ability to quote large portions of Scripture. Remember, "knowledge puffs up, but love builds up" (1 Corinthians 8:1). (This verse provides an indication of at least one attribute you *do* need as a small group leader!)

Latoya Leader

Believe it or not, leadership is not the most essential spiritual gift a small group leader needs. You can use different spiritual gifts to lead a life-changing group, depending on the type, personality, and purpose of your group. God provides each person in the group with spiritual gifts to utilize in the functioning of the group. Latoya's job is to facilitate the usage of those various gifts.

Teasley Teacher

"Let the word of Christ dwell in you richly as you teach and admonish one another with all wisdom" (Colossians 3:16). In a small group, everyone is involved in teaching one another. As a small group leader, Teasley needs to be more of a shepherd than teacher. He does not have to be the group's "Bible answer man."

Neither do you.

THE HEART OF THE MATTER

Leader, what are you known for? Your knowledge? Leadership ability? Facilitation skills? Or that you are one who, it is obvious, spends time with Jesus? God needs many more regular folks—nonprofessional Christians—people like you who will be with him and allow him to make you into the leader he needs you to be.

Eddie Educated

While a good education does not preclude Eddie from small group leadership, it is also not a prerequisite. Eddie's heart is much more vital than Eddie's education.

Chris "Super-Stud" Christian

In Jesus' day, the Pharisees were the super studs of the religious world. Jesus' followers, on the other hand, were simple, run-of-the-mill average Joes. Jesus spent time with some everyday people and made them extraordinary. Chris does not have to be the perfect Christian—whatever that means!—to lead well.

WHAT IS THE SMALL GROUP LEADER'S ROLE?

Perhaps the best job description for a small group leader comes straight off the pages of the Bible, from 1 Peter 5:2-4. The writer, the apostle Peter, knew what he was talking about, too. Peter followed the best small group leader ever for several years. Look closely at this passage, and underline the words or phrases that you think describe a small group leader.

> Be shepherds of God's flock that is under your care, serving as overseers—not because you must, but because you are willing, as God wants you to be; not greedy for money, but eager to serve; not lording it over those entrusted to you, but being examples to the flock. And when the Chief Shepherd appears, you will receive the crown of glory that will never fade away (1 Peter 5:2-4).

WiSe Words

This passage was written to elders in the first-century church. These church leaders were called to shepherd the churches in a particular city (i.e., the church in Ephesus) or churches that met in specific homes. This passage also applies to what a small group leader is called to do in today's church.

We'll come back to this passage often throughout this book. It reveals the roles and responsibilities God has given you as a small group leader.

DO YOU HAVE WHAT IT TAKES?

Do you have what it takes to be a small group leader? Depending on your perspective you can answer this question two different ways:

NO: *You* do not have what it takes…on your own, under your own power, with your own intellect. That's why it's so vital to remember that Jesus is the real leader of "your" group. "'Not by might nor by power, but by my Spirit,' says the Lord Almighty" (Zechariah 4:6).

YES: Don't forget that Jesus calls unschooled, ordinary men and women to follow him and then turns them into world changers. If you follow the best small group leader ever, he will use you to do extraordinary things. Don't sell yourself short. Say, "I can do everything through him who gives me strength" (Philippians 4:13).

By God's power, you can do this, but you have to start by first seeking after him. That's the topic for Chapter 2.

NOW WHAT?

✔ Who is the best small group leader you've ever known?

✔ What qualities did that person have that made him or her a good leader?

❏ Knowledge ❏ Love

❏ Facilitating Skills ❏ Character

❏ Speaking Ability ❏ Listening Ability

✔ What have you learned about leadership from this person?

Go ahead, you can write in your book!

Seek

What do you want to be known for? Think about this for a moment before reading on. What would you want people to say about you when you die? What do you want written in your obituary? Go ahead, write it here!

At different stages of my life I would have responded to that question differently. As a kid growing up in Cincinnati, I wanted to be known as a great athlete, a Hall of Fame baseball player like Johnny Bench or Pete Rose. (Now I'd have to just say Johnny Bench.)

My athletic career was not that spectacular. I accumulated lots of trophies, but mostly because I happened to be on some good teams. I did get three individual awards. In basketball I got the award for best defense…which went to the kid who never scored a basket. In baseball one year, I got the "Most Spirited Player" trophy…which went to the kid who sat on the bench and cheered on the rest of the team.

My favorite award was the Most Improved Player…which went to the kid who didn't stink quite as bad as the year before. The trophy had the initials "MIP" on the plaque. I overheard my mom telling all her friends I got the "Most Important Player" award. At least my mom appreciated my talent!

In college I would have said I wanted to be well-known, period. Didn't matter for what, just popular. I had gotten about as far as I could in most athletics, so, just for fun, I went out for the cheerleading squad at the University of Cincinnati. I figured at the very least I'd get to meet a few pretty girls. On a fluke, I made the squad, three years straight. I was proud to be a "big man on campus" with my cool letter jacket. I was "known."

In my twenties, I would have said I wanted to be remembered for being successful. I wanted to climb the ladder of success, until the ladder and everything else in my life fell out from under me. That's when I gave my life to Christ, and everything changed. Well, almost everything.

Since becoming a Christian eighteen years ago, if I was really honest, I might have said I want to be well-known and successful as a Christian writer, small group "expert," or minister. At times, in my more reflective moments, I might have said I want to be remembered as a good husband, a great dad, and a trusted friend.

Today, I want to be like Enoch. You don't hear too many people say that, do you? People will say they want to have the faith of Abraham or the power of Moses or the wisdom of Solomon. But Enoch? Who's Enoch?

I love what Genesis 5:22-24 says about him: "Enoch lived in close fellowship with God for another 300 years… Then one day he disappeared, because God took him" (NLT).

No, I don't want to live another 300 years! And it's not at all necessary to just disappear without dying, unless it's the rapture, of course. But I do want to live in close fellowship with God throughout what's left of my life, and then for God to take me when he's ready.

Enoch had a heart for God, and small group leadership starts with your heart. It starts with your relationship with God—seeking after him.

One of the key attributes from 1 Peter 5:2-4 for small group leaders is that you are an "example to the flock." That is why it is so critical that you are, first of all, a man or woman after God's heart. It's why the most important thing you can do as a leader is to earnestly seek God every day.

THE INSIDE STUFF OF SMALL GROUP LEADERSHIP

If it were your job to recruit a team of small group leaders, what would you look for? What would matter most?

- ❏ Facilitation skills
- ❏ Spiritual gift of leadership
- ❏ Previous involvement in a small group
- ❏ Bible knowledge
- ❏ Daily quiet time
- ❏ Relational abilities
- ❏ Dynamic personality
- ❏ Ability to use a DVD player
- ❏ Holiness, piety
- ❏ Whoever says yes when you ask

How would the best small group leader ever answer that question? I believe he would say something like, "Don't look at the outward appearance; look inside" (see 1 Samuel 16:7).

THE HEART OF THE MATTER

The USA Men's Olympic Basketball Team, known as the "Dream Team," consisted of some of the best NBA players and a few elite college players.

When Jesus selected his team, it was perhaps the most important team ever assembled. Their job: to communicate the most significant message in history to the entire world. It was a do-or-die mission. They do it...or the whole world dies spiritually. But Jesus didn't select a dream team. He called a rag-tag assortment of very average men. And, he said, he would make them into what they needed to become.

Actually, you don't have to conjecture what Jesus would have looked for in leaders. When he invited some folks to be part of his group, he was calling future leaders. "The plan was that they would be with Jesus, and he would send them out" (Mark 3:14, *The Message*).

If Jesus would have recruited future leaders who looked good by outward appearances he probably would have picked some of the religious leaders of the day. They were all about outward appearances, which is what frustrated Jesus the most about them. These leaders had skills and abilities and giftedness. They had knowledge and holiness and piety above almost everyone around. They were highly disciplined in spiritual practices. But there was something missing on the inside.

Small group leadership starts with your relationship with God—seeking after him with all your heart, soul, strength, and mind.

The Best Small Group Leader Ever Said . . .

"How terrible it will be for you teachers of religious law and you Pharisees. Hypocrites! You are like whitewashed tombs—beautiful on the outside but filled on the inside with dead people's bones and all sorts of impurity. You try to look like upright people outwardly, but inside your hearts are filled with hypocrisy and lawlessness."

—Matthew 23:27, 28 (*NLT*)

Gut-Level Leadership

The best small group leader ever is a perfect model for us. Jesus' priority was his relationship with his Father. He said and did and taught only what his Father had given him. Henri Nouwen once pointed out that Jesus spent about 50 percent of his time in solitude with the Father, about 40 percent building community with the twelve, and about 10 percent "doing ministry."[1] How does that match up with your life?

"I assure you, the Son can do nothing by himself. He does only what he sees the Father doing. Whatever the Father does, the Son also does."

—John 5:19, NLT

In *Experiencing God*, Blackaby and King also describe Jesus—and godly leaders today—spending abundant amounts of time seeking God. These leaders have discerned the difference between activity *for* God and the activity *of* God. Jesus never ran ahead of God. Instead, before making any decisions or starting any new ministry work, he spent time with his Father, maybe days on end, waiting on God to show him exactly what to do next.

Joel Comiskey's survey of more than 700 small group leaders in eight countries revealed that the biggest factor in the "success" of small group leaders was not their gender, social status, education, personality type, or skills. Rather, it was the leader's devotional life. He found that those who spent 90 minutes or more in devotions (prayer, Bible study, etc.) a day multiplied their groups twice as much as those who spent less than 30 minutes.[2] Comiskey says the correlation is logical. "During quiet times alone with the living God, the [small group] leader hears God's voice and receives His guidance…Group members respond to a leader who hears from God and knows the way."[3]

Jesus modeled seeking and following God for us. As our Leader and Savior, he is our Good Shepherd who calls us by name and is waiting to lead us (John 10:3, 4). Are you quiet and still enough to hear his voice?

Let me encourage you as you read this to get gut-level honest with yourself. Where are you in your relationship with God? Are you…

➤ **Walking right behind him; his voice is crystal clear**

➤ **Meandering along toward the back of the crowd, his voice is like bad cell-phone service— sometimes clear, but lots of dropped calls**

➤ **Running this way and that; I hear lots of voices, lots of noise—his voice is indistinguishable**

The biggest factor in the "success" of small group leaders is their devotional life.

➤ **Stuck in a rut; I haven't heard his voice in a while**

➤ **Other:** _____

Before going any further in this book—before considering how you can become a more effective leader—you must get honest with yourself, and with God, on this. Then, there's the next step. You'll need to share this with someone else. Get gut-level honest with another person: someone from your group, a church leader, or a good, trusted friend. I'm asking you to be vulnerable, authentic. Until you get gut-level honest with yourself, God, and at least one other person, you cannot become a more effective leader and guide an effective, growing small group.

GO AWAY TO GET INSIDE

How do you get to a place where you can hear God's voice? The only way is to spend time alone with him. I fear that small group leaders sometimes miss this vital point. Most leaders are busy people, busy with jobs, families, churches, and small groups. We're all community junkies. We love spending time with other people. But, as Dietrich Bonhoeffer said, solitude and community go hand in hand for spiritually healthy people and groups.

Jesus modeled this for us as well. "One day soon afterward Jesus went to a mountain to pray, and he prayed to God all night. At daybreak he called together all of his disciples and chose twelve of them to be apostles." Before Jesus did anything, he spent time alone with the Father. In fact, Luke 5:16 says, "Jesus often withdrew to lonely places and prayed."

My sense is that, as Christian leaders, we talk about this a lot, but not many of us really slow our lives down enough to actually do it. However there are a few exceptions.

Bob Cherry, the senior minister at the church where I serve, takes a break every July to pray, listen to God, and plan out the next year. A couple years ago, he sensed a need to spend even more time away, so he took a sabbatical and spent several months away in the mountains and by the ocean listening to God and allowing God to show him a direction for our church.

David Yonggi Cho, pastor of the largest church in the recorded history of the church, attributes the tremendous growth of his church to prayer. In 1984,

> **THE BEST SMALL GROUP LEADER EVER SAID...**
>
> "But seek first his kingdom and his righteousness, and all these things will be given to you as well."
>
> —Matthew 6:33

when the church was averaging 12,000 new converts a month, he wrote a book titled, *Prayer: Key to Revival*. A staff pastor at this church said, "More important than all the growth-producing practices at our church is the presence and reality of spiritual empowerment. As we join with God in prayer for ourselves and for others, He gives us *His* power, wisdom, and strength."

Karen Hurston, who grew up in this church, says the typical small group leader prays an hour a day, more than half of them attend one all-night prayer meeting each week, many fast for specific unbelievers to come to a saving relationship with Christ, and most make three to five prayer visits to members' homes each week.[4] These leaders are committed to their groups and committed to God in prayer! Some of their small groups spend two-thirds of their meeting time in prayer.

Joel Comiskey shares the story of Ray Prior, president of the Borden Corporation, one of the largest business structures in America. Someone asked him how he led such a large company. He said, "Each morning when I wake up, I meet with the Lord and begin to listen to His voice. In that period of time, I ask Him to bring to my mind the needs of the key men who report directly to me. As I think about their weaknesses, I plan my day."[5]

Spending time with God is your primary priority as a small group leader. But this will not just happen. You must make it happen! Use these questions to plan your getaway.

GETAWAY PLANNING!

How Often will I get away alone with God? (weekly, monthly, quarterly, yearly?)

How Long will I spend alone with God?

When will I get away to be alone with God? (Be specific!)

Where will I go?

What provisions do I need to make for getting away? (asking permission, child care, financial arrangements, place to stay, etc.)

I don't get away for solitude with God often enough, but when I do, I spend a day in the woods, especially a woods with a creek or near a lake. I feel particularly close to God there. I plan on either hiking or taking my mountain bike, but only as a way to get to a solitary place. These times are refreshing to my own soul, they remind me of the calling God has placed on my life, and they revive me for the ministry God has called me to do. More than anything else, during these times I sense God's presence and power, and I realize that he really is pursuing me and leading me.

Don't miss this! God is either pursuing you, trying to draw you closer to him, or he is leading you, walking in front of you to guide you (John 10:4). When you belong to him, he does whatever you need at the time, as your Good Shepherd.

"As the deer pants for streams of water, so my soul pants for you, O God. My soul thirsts for God, for the living God. When can I go and meet with God?"

—Psalm 42:1, 2

One of my favorite places is the woods and the creek right behind my backyard. I've built a mountain bike trail and enjoy all kinds of adventures—alone and with my kids—back there.

One of my favorite spots is a tree bridge. Two huge trees have fallen across the creek. One is a little higher than the other, creating a perfect chair where I can sit and rest my feet. It's a great place to read my Bible or just sit and pray.

Another spot is a large rock in the middle of the stream. It's mossy and soft and just the right shape for sitting and relaxing. It's an incredibly beautiful spot, where a side stream cascades down a hill. Lots of flat rocks and little waterfalls create the rhythmical sound of babbling water.

I was sitting there this morning, taking in the vast beauty of God's creation all around me, when I looked down. There, right between my feet, was a little plant growing in the moss. It had tiny white flowers, smaller than the size of the head of a pin, but incredibly beautiful and intricate. I sat there and stared at it for maybe fifteen minutes. It was a gift to me from God, a reminder that I needed to look not only at the big picture (something I do a lot), but stop and notice the little things in life as well.

I have a deadline looming (for this book!) and I've been working on it nonstop for a while. God knew exactly what I needed, and he provided it. He pursued me and drew me closer to him, as I slowed down enough to notice. God desires leaders who seek him earnestly, know his voice, and know his heart— leaders who respond to him and walk in close fellowship with him every day. Leaders like that are ones who are experiencing the abundant life.

LIFE IN ALL ITS FULLNESS

Life to the full, the abundant life, more and better life than you've ever dreamed of, everything you need. These are ways different Bible versions say the same thing.

You cannot lead a small group to experience the fullness of God's love and grace unless you are living it yourself. In Matthew 11:28-30, Jesus presents three ways to respond to his offer of abundant life:

> **THE BEST SMALL GROUP LEADER EVER SAID...**
>
> "The thief comes only to steal and kill and destroy; I have come that they may have life, and have it to the full."
>
> —John 10:10

1. Come to me...and I will give you rest.

Life to the full comes only through Jesus. Your response to him is to seek God and stay connected to him.

When you come to Jesus, as his first disciples did, you give your life to him, commit to following him, and let him mold you into what he wants you to be. When you come to him, he gives you rest, especially from legalism—following all the rules to be right with God. The abundant life is far more than living a holy and blameless life. The Pharisees worked hard at living like that, but their lives were empty. They were living religious, rule-keeping lives, but not full lives. When your life is empty—when you have not invited Jesus to take up residence in your life—you are in danger of all kinds of other things—evil things—coming in and taking up residence. Being religious will not fill you up. It will leave you only empty and vulnerable. Only Jesus has the power to really fill you—to give you life to the full.

2. Take my yoke upon you.

This next step as you become more mature is the place of surrender to God. Not only do you accept Jesus as your Savior so you gain peace and eternal life, but you also know him as leader of your life, surrendering to his ways and his will. This is the place of service, using the gifts God has given you to administer his grace. Remember that the "yoke" Jesus gives you always fits perfectly! (I will discuss the subjects of surrender and serving in much more detail in Chapters 3 and 5.)

WiSe WorDs

"Each one should use whatever gift he has received to serve others, faithfully administering God's grace in its various forms."
—1 Peter 4:10

The abundant life is not the same as the "good life" that so many people run after. It is not necessarily a life free from pain, sadness, difficulties, or other burdens that people face every day. Jesus does not give us these difficult burdens, but he also does not always take away the difficulties and challenges we face in life.

The apostle Paul described how to live life to the full in Philippians 4:11, 12, when he talked about learning the secret of being content, regardless of the circumstances. The abundant life is a life of joy—a joy that can be possessed regardless of the circumstances. It is a life of rest from burdens—a rest that only Jesus can give you. It is a life of freedom—freedom from the burdensome, ill-fitting yoke of rule-keeping.

> The abundant life is a life of joy—a joy that can be possessed regardless of the circumstances.

That reminds me of a story I read about a man who was released from jail at 12:01 a.m. At 12:09 a.m. he was spotted climbing over a chain link fence, back onto the jail grounds, and attempting to pass a cigarette to an inmate through a steel grate covering a window. At 12:10 A.M. the man was back in custody, charged with illegal entry into a prison facility and disorderly conduct. True story! Can you identify at all with this stupid criminal? The apostle Paul wrote about all of us:

> Christ has set us free to live a free life. So take your stand! Never again let anyone put a harness of slavery on you. I am emphatic about this. The moment any one of you submits to circumcision or any other rule-keeping system, at that same moment Christ's hard-won gift of freedom is squandered… . I suspect you would never intend this, but this is what happens. When you attempt to live by your own religious plans and projects, you are cut off from Christ, you fall out of grace. Galatians 5:1-4, *The Message*.

What do you allow to take away your freedom? It's probably not circumcision, as it was for Paul's friends. You may not literally be breaking into jail, like our stupid criminal, but all of us, at one time or another, give up the freedom Jesus has given us, choosing to live as a prisoner.

I want to encourage you, leader to leader—don't return to the prison cell of living by a list of do's and don'ts. As a spiritual leader, you are a model of the type of life God wants everyone to live. In Paul's day, the Judaizers taught that believers needed to become Jews first (by being circumcised) in order to become Christians. These spiritual leaders were not only living as prisoners themselves, they were trying to lead other Christians back into bondage. Be careful, then, not to be like these "agitators," as Paul calls them (Galatians 5:12). Rather, live your life in freedom in Christ!

> ## Caution
>
> In Matthew 13, Jesus tells his small group a story about a farmer scattering seed on different types of soils. The seed is the Good News of the life Jesus came to give. But many things can keep you from living that life: obstacles, strongholds, worries, busyness, misdirection, confusion between the "good life" and the abundant life. Jesus gives it freely, but you cannot always receive it. Your heart has to be fertile—ready to receive the good seed God wants to plant there.

Jesus reminds us often in the gospels about the costs involved in coming to him. These involve the possibility of losing your family members, finances, job, position in life, maybe even life itself. How can these "yokes" be easy and not burdensome? Only by putting your total trust in Jesus and learning from him how to live.

3. Learn from me.

Part of the ongoing process of experiencing the abundant life more is to learn from Jesus how to live. He teaches you by his example, his Holy Spirit, and his Word. As you yield to his will, you learn how to live life his way.

The best small group leader ever lived life to the full himself. So he is a perfect model for us. In John 4:34, Jesus said, "My food is to do the will of him who sent me and to finish his work." Part of living the abundant life is living your life for God, not yourself, doing his will, and living according to the purpose he has given you.

In Matthew 24 and 25, Jesus emphasized and re-emphasized the need to stay alert. The abundant life is lived with a constant focus on Jesus (Colossians 3:2). It's all too easy to shift your attention elsewhere. Jesus is encouraging and warning you to stay focused on him.

When you are seeking him and focused on him, you can live life the way he wants you to live it: abundantly…actually, super abundantly!

LIVING AN OVERFLOWING LIFE

In John 10:10, the word for *full* or *abundantly* actually means *overfilled* or *superabundantly*. Think of a glass of water filled to the brim. That's what I used to think of when I thought of "life to the full." But it's more than that! It's a life that is overflowing the glass. Your life can't even contain it all! What Jesus pours into your life he intends to overflow into the lives of those all around you—your family, neighbors, co-workers, and yes, your small group. That's why it is critical that you are living the abundant life yourself.

Of course, Jesus was the perfect example of someone living this superabundant life. He taught his disciples how to live by intentionally letting his life overflow into theirs over time.

WiSe WordS

Read Psalm 23, "the shepherd's psalm," with the abundant life in mind. God promises life to the full regardless of the valleys in life. But he promises even more than that. The psalmist says, "My cup overflows" (v. 5).

For three years the disciples followed Jesus everywhere. He taught them. Showed them. Modeled it for them. Prayed for them. And as you follow the story through the gospels, you know that these guys just didn't get it most of the time. Oh, there would be a flash of brilliance, a hint of promise, but minutes later they'd look like the "uneducated idiots" most of the world saw them as. Dumb fishermen. Scurrilous government workers. Insolent rebels. What did Jesus see in these guys that no one else saw? I think he saw potential and promise. He knew that when push came to shove—and it would—what the Father had been pouring into Jesus for three years, which was naturally overflowing into their lives as well, would then begin to flow out of their lives. Jesus staked *everything* on this.

Uneducated Idiots: In Acts 4:13, the Jewish rulers called Peter and John "unschooled, ordinary men." The word the ruler's used for "ordinary" in the original language was *idiotai*. "Unschooled, ordinary men" is just a polite way of saying "uneducated idiots"!

After three years, they definitely did not look like world changers. But that, of course, is exactly what they became. Somehow, through the midst of what seemed like the biggest tragedy of all—the death of their leader—they pulled off what looked like the impossible. The religious leaders, who thought they had gotten rid of the "problem," had a sinking suspicion that it really wasn't over. There was something special, something *dangerous*, about these "uneducated idiots." People were amazed.

How did Jesus do it? How were these uneducated idiots transformed? There were several key ingredients: prayer, authentic community, and the indwelling of the Holy Spirit, for starters. And these are huge, of course. But the thing that people noticed most was that these uneducated idiots had been with Jesus.

The discipline of "remaining" is vital for the disciple's life. Jesus spoke little to his followers about spiritual exercises or spiritual disciplines, even though they were undoubtedly a big part of their religious heritage. Instead, Jesus called them to come and see (John 1:39), come and follow me (Mark 1:16-20), come and be with me (Mark 3:13-14), and remain

Wise Words

"The members of the council were amazed when they saw the boldness of Peter and John, for they could see that they were ordinary men who had had no special training. They also recognized them as men who had been with Jesus."

—Acts 4:13, *NLT*

in me (John 15:7-8). Jesus did many things in his three-year earthly ministry, but the one constant was his presence with the disciples.

Nothing is more vital to spiritual leadership than being with Jesus—connected to him, remaining in him, abiding in him. Remember that you are *not* the vine that supplies all the nutrients for growth and fruitfulness in your group members' lives. You are one of the branches that are dependent on the true vine, Jesus (John 15:1-17). His life flows into you, which naturally overflows into your group members, and then continues to flow from them into their spheres of influence.

When you remain connected to him, you will produce much fruit—abundant fruit, fruit that overflows the containers, fruit that will last. But apart from him, you can do nothing. That's quite a difference!

This overflowing life provides a good definition for a small group leader:

A small group leader is a group member who goes first.

As a good shepherd, you lead your sheep (John 10:3, 4). You don't drive them from behind. You lead by going first in and modeling the abundant life by…

- ➤ **SEEKING GOD**
- ➤ **LIVING IN AUTHENTIC COMMUNITY**
- ➤ **IMPACTING YOUR WORLD**

These are the three vital relationships that are part of living life abundantly. They are the essential pursuits of every abundant living small group. I will continue to discuss these values throughout the rest of this book. Your job as the leader is to go first in pursuing each of these relationships, just as Jesus did. Your role is to be an example to the flock that is under your care (1 Peter 5:2, 3).

To live the kind of life I've discussed in this chapter, one of the first things you'll need to learn to do everyday of your life—and this is something that must be modeled for others—is to surrender. That's the topic of Chapter 3.

THE HEART OF THE MATTER

"We will teach what we know, but we will reproduce what we are."

—Familiar Proverb

NOW WHAT?

In Ephesians 3:14-21, the apostle Paul prayed for the Ephesian church's spiritual empowerment. In your own Bible, read this passage, and then pray that prayer for each of your group members (starting with yourself).

Pray that Christ will be more and more at home in your own heart, so that you are living the superabundant life Jesus came to give—a life that overflows into the lives of your group members. Pray that Jesus will be more at home in the lives of your members, so that they may also be filled to the measure of all the fullness of God.

A student is not above his teacher, but everyone who is fully trained will be like his teacher.
—Luke 6:40

---

[1]*Leadership*, Spring 1995.

[2]Joel Comiskey, *Home Cell Group Explosion* (Houston, Texas: TOUCH Outreach Ministries, 1998), 26-36.

[3]Ibid, 34.

[4]Karen Hurston, "The Small Groups Behind the World's Largest Church," *Strategies for Today's Leader*, Spring 1999, 16, 17.

[5]Joel Comiskey, *Leadership Explosion* (Houston, Texas: TOUCH Publications, 2000), 46.

Surrender

3

You are seeking God, striving to live life to the full. The next step in becoming more like the best small group leader ever is not easy, but it is vital. Until you learn to surrender, you cannot realistically live out the rest of the leadership values in this book and become more like the best leader ever.

The word *surrender*, as it relates to yielding one's will to God, is seldom used in

> ✓
> ## Surrender:
> *the complete giving up of [one's] own will and subjecting…thoughts, ideas, and deeds to the will and teachings of a divine power or deity (Wikipedia.org).*

Scripture, yet the idea flows through God's Word from the start. Adam and Eve gave in to sin as they chose their own wills rather than surrendering to God's. They yielded to Satan's scheme. This pattern has continued to repeat itself through history.

SURRENDER YOUR WILL

Living life to the full does not mean getting everything you want. It means knowing and following the will of God. That takes surrender—total abandonment to God, forsaking the security of meeting your own needs by your own means. Surrender demands faith in a God who will never fail you. It is an act of the will.

Caution

Men don't like the word *surrender*. To many of us guys it means "I lose." Like many men, I'm competitive; losing is not in my vocabulary! But *surrender* in the sense that I'm using it here does not mean capitulation or waving the white flag. It means intentionally sacrificing myself for the good of others. It's *Saving Private Ryan.* It's the firemen in the World Trade Center. It's Jesus at the cross.

Jesus provided us a perfect example of surrender, first by emptying himself of the privileges, power, and prerogatives of divinity by coming into this world as a human (Philippians 2:7), then by how he lived, and finally by laying down his life for us. Jesus modeled it so that we will lay down our lives for one another (1 John 3:16).

I love reading through the Gospel of John and seeing Jesus' heart for how he did ministry. Over and over he says, I do nothing on my own. I do only what the Father tells me to do. I say only the words the Father gives me to say. Jesus was voluntarily submissive to his Father and his will.

> ### THE BEST SMALL GROUP LEADER EVER SAID...
>
> "For I have come down from Heaven not to do my will but to do the will of him who sent me."
> —John 6:38

At the end of his ministry on earth, Jesus said he had accomplished everything the Father had given him to do (John 17:4). Up to that point, what had he accomplished? If I had been a reporter for the *Palestine Times,* I probably would have labeled Jesus a failure. He had failed to win Jewish leaders and most of the Jewish people over, he had not cured all the diseases or stopped any of the regional conflicts. Even his closest followers still argued over who was greatest, and most of them ran and hid at Jesus' most desperate hour. Yet, Jesus said he had accomplished everything the Father had given him to do.

"Submission is a love word, not a control word. Submission means letting someone love you, teach you, or influence you."[1]

—from *The Ascent of a Leader*

What *you* think you should make happen or what *others* might expect of you may be diametrically opposed to what God has given you to do. What you are called to do is to live a submissive, surrendered life to God each and every day. As for me, above all else, I'd like to be able to say at the end of my life, "Father, I brought you glory here on earth by doing everything you told me to do." That's going to take a change in ownership.

A CHANGE IN OWNERSHIP

In my twenties I worked as a retail store manager. One of my jobs was to go into stores that were losing money and turn them around. The first thing I would do was to put two signs in the front window: "Under New Management" and "Now Hiring." I usually fired most of the staff and then hired a new team and instilled new values and attitudes. Not everyone liked my tactics, of course, but it worked. To my surprise, the president of the company called me one day to congratulate me and ask how I was doing it. He expressed some concern over what he considered my extreme measures, but he liked the results!

When you became a Christian, you came under new ownership. That might mean some drastic changes; getting rid of old behaviors and ways of thinking. Out with the old values and attitudes; in with the new ways of living. *Purpose Driven Daily Devotion* writer John Fischer discussed our new ownership. I like the way he put it:

WiSe WordS

"You are not your own; you were bought at a price."

— 1 Corinthians 6:19, 20

> What does it mean to not belong to myself? I can think of a few things. It means that I should probably do a lot of consulting with my new owner. There is more to consider than just me and what I want to do; there is God and what He wants me to do. ...but in all instances it is the attitude of the heart that is most important. It is a submissive attitude toward God that He is looking for—what the Old Testament calls a broken and contrite heart. It's being always open and teachable because I realize my new owner has a different way of looking at things than what comes natural for me. In fact, over time I begin to realize what comes natural for me is often my biggest problem.[2]

"The fact that God can bring character development and personal growth out of any situation is conditional on people's willingness to submit to God's will. God is sovereign over every life, but those who yield their will to him will be shaped according to his purposes."

—Henry and Richard Blackaby[3]

This is one of the best things I've learned in life—and certainly one of the hardest to learn: *It's not about me. It's all about him.* But, like Adam and Eve, I so easily forget that fact and, again and again, act for myself.

As a spiritual seeker nearly 20 years ago, I was profoundly influenced by the little booklets produced by Campus Crusade. My niece, Julie, used "The Four Spiritual Laws" to introduce me to a relationship with Jesus as my Savior. A little later, I came across "Would You Like to Know God Personally," which helped me to more fully know Jesus as my Lord. Three little circles in that booklet challenged my viewpoint on life. And they still do.[4]

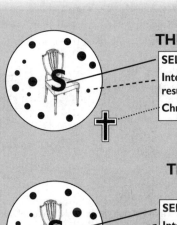

THE SELF-DIRECTED LIFE

SELF is on the throne

Interests are directed by self, resulting in discord, frustration

Christ is outside the life

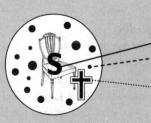

THE SELF-DIRECTED RELIGIOUS LIFE

SELF is on the throne

Interests are directed by self, resulting in discord, frustration

Christ is in the life, but not on the throne

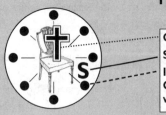

THE CHRIST-DIRECTED SURRENDERED LIFE

CHRIST is on the throne

Self is yielding to Christ

Interests are directed by Christ, resulting in harmony with God's plan

I had breakfast this morning with a guy from our church who is a new Christian. I showed him these three circles, and he admitted he's still living life in the second one. That may not be unusual for a new Christian, but it's very sad when those who have known Jesus as their Savior are still living there.

Life to the full can only be lived in the third circle. Leading a small group should only be done in that circle as well. I'm learning that living in the third circle is an everyday decision—a decision of the will. But that decision will certainly bring conflict.

Even the best small group leader ever dealt with this conflict. Before he began his ministry, he battled it out with Satan in the desert. Of course, Jesus submitted to the Word of God and did not yield to Satan. At the end of his earthly ministry, in the Garden of Gethsemane, Jesus again faced the conflict head-on. His response to his Father: "Your will must be done, not mine" (Luke 22:42, *God's Word*).

caution

Like the stores I turned around, the change in management of your life will create some battles. As Fischer puts it, "It used to be just me. Now I have me and the Spirit and we may not always be in sync."

> For we do not have a high priest who is unable to sympathize with our weaknesses, but we have one who has been tempted in every way, just as we are—yet was without sin.
>
> —Hebrews 4:15

The fact that Jesus battled this conflict—the fact that he even had to say, "not mine"—means that Jesus had a will that was sometimes prone to not be the same as the Father's will. Their wills—like yours and mine—were not always in sync. I know that might sound sacrilegious, but it is biblical and it helps me, at least, to know that Jesus dealt with the same temptations as I do, yet did not sin.

You and I have the same spiritual power that was available to Jesus in that desert and in the garden. We have the power of his Spirit within us to help us fight this battle and not yield to sin.

You are under new management, and he wants you to live your new life to the full. But that's not all—you also have a new citizenship.

A Change in Citizenship

When you became a Christian, you took a new citizenship. No longer do you belong to this world. Your citizenship is now in the kingdom of Heaven. Comparing non-Christians and Christians of his day, the apostle Paul commented, "Their mind is on earthly things. But our citizenship is in Heaven" (Philippians 3:19, 20). Being a citizen of Heaven means a change in values and priorities, from the world's systems and standards to those of your new king. It means a change in rules. You now live by God's Word, not by the principles of the world.

Jesus is a perfect example of someone who lived as a citizen in Heaven while in this world. He was not of this world (John 8:23; 17:14, 16), and he reminded his disciples that neither were they (15:19). Neither the religious leaders, the disciples, nor Pilate understood Jesus' true citizenship even though the kingdom of Heaven was one of

Caution

No one sneaks across the border or bribes their way into citizenship in Heaven. It is a free gift with many privileges and opportunities, and yet, once you're in, responsibilities come with being a citizen of Heaven. Make sure you count the cost!

his favorite subjects to talk about. He told Pilate, "My kingdom is not of this world. ...my kingdom is from another place" (John 18:36).

You are called to live in this world and yet not be a citizen of it. Like Abraham, who "made his home in the promised land like a stranger in a foreign country; he lived in tents. ...For he was looking forward to the city with foundations, whose architect and builder is God" (Hebrews 11:9, 10).

So here are a couple tough questions to consider and perhaps discuss with your small group: Do you live in this world like a foreigner or a native? Are you living your life in "tents," not putting down roots because you know this is not your home, or are you settled in? Are you living in comfort here or in hope for your future home?

Part of living as a citizen of Heaven is surrendering your own desires so that you can carry out the will of the king. But how do you know his will? The answer is clear, even if it is not easy: "Do not conform any longer to the pattern of this world, but be transformed by the renewing of your mind. Then you will be able to test and approve what God's will is" (Romans 12:2). When you surrender the things the world offers, no longer conforming to it's ways, and when you allow your mind to be changed into a new way of thinking—a kingdom mindset—*then* God shows you his will for your life.

Try this today. Use Romans 12:2 as an acid test for every decision you make, everything you do, whatever enters your mind, every emotion that you feel. Does your decision, thought, emotion, or action cause you to conform to the world's ways or be transformed to God's ways? This will take full attention and strict discipline, but it will help you know and understand God's will.

> "Our sphere of life is not this earth, but Heaven; and the things that attract us and excite us belong to Heaven, not to earth."
>
> —Warren Wiersbe

What specific changes do you need to make to live as a citizen of Heaven? Take time to reflect on each of the Bible passages in the table on pages 32 and 33. What do you still need to surrender, and what are your new responsibilities?

What changes do you need to make to live as a citizen of Heaven?

One more thing in regard to your new citizenship. The king—the one who has made you a citizen of his kingdom—has given you a significant role. While you are here in this world, he wants you to represent him as his ambassador. He has given you the message about this kingdom, and he wants you to tell everyone you know about it (see 2 Corinthians 5:16-21). And—take note—this is not optional if you are a citizen of Heaven. I'll discuss this more in Chapter 5.

VERSE	PASSAGE	SURRENDER	RESPONSI-BILITIES
MATTHEW 6:19-21, 33	Do not store up for yourselves treasures on earth, where moth and rust destroy, and where thieves break in and steal. But store up for yourselves treasures in heaven, where moth and rust do not destroy, and where thieves do not break in and steal. For where your treasure is, there your heart will be also. ...But seek first his kingdom and his righteousness, and all these things will be given to you as well.		
ROMANS 7:4-6	You also died to the law through the body of Christ, that you might belong to another, to him who was raised from the dead, in order that we might bear fruit to God. For when we were controlled by the sinful nature, the sinful passions aroused by the law were at work in our bodies, so that we bore fruit for death. But now, by dying to what once bound us, we have been released from the law so that we serve in the new way of the Spirit, and not in the old way of the written code.		

VERSE	PASSAGE	SURRENDER	RESPONSI-BILITIES
EPHESIANS 2:1-10	As for you, you were dead in your transgressions and sins, in which you used to live when you followed the ways of this world and of the ruler of the kingdom of the air, the spirit who is now at work in those who are disobedient. All of us also lived among them at one time, gratifying the cravings of our sinful nature and following its desires and thoughts. Like the rest, we were by nature objects of wrath. But because of his great love for us, God, who is rich in mercy, made us alive with Christ even when we were dead in transgressions—it is by grace you have been saved. And God raised us up with Christ and seated us with him in the heavenly realms in Christ Jesus, in order that in the coming ages he might show the incomparable riches of his grace, expressed in his kindness to us in Christ Jesus. ...For we are God's workmanship, created in Christ Jesus to do good works, which God prepared in advance for us to do.		
COLOSSIANS 3:1-3	Since, then, you have been raised with Christ, set your hearts on things above, where Christ is seated at the right hand of God. Set your minds on things above, not on earthly things. For you died, and your life is now hidden with Christ in God.		

If you are surrendering your will, you're off to a good start! That decision inexplicably leads to the next one, to surrender your assignment.

SURRENDER YOUR ASSIGNMENT

God gives the assignment. Your job is to surrender to his will and purpose for your life.

If his will and purpose is for you to lead a small group or a church or a movement, then lead diligently (Romans 12:8)!

If his will and purpose is for you to sweep floors or be a Christian lawyer or be a missionary to Iraq or to *fill in the blank*, then do it with all your heart, as serving the Lord, not men (Colossians 3:23).

> **THE BEST SMALL GROUP LEADER EVER SAID...**
>
> "But among you it should be quite different. Whoever wants to be a leader among you must be your servant."
>
> —Mark 10:43, *NLT*

When you took on a new citizenship, your way to the top changed drastically. Citizens of the world's system *aspire* to leadership. Citizens of Heaven are *assigned* to leadership.

THE HEART OF THE MATTER

You assume the role of a leader "not because you must, but because you are willing, as God wants you to be" (1 Peter 5:2). Are you a small group leader because someone recruited you or there is a shortage of leaders, or because you have been called by God? You will recognize that calling because of the spiritual gifts or the passion he has given you or because, well, you just know he has called you to shepherd a group of people. You know it because you are a sheep and he is your shepherd. When he called you, you heard his voice.

APPOINTED, NOT RECRUITED

Leading a small group (or anything else in the church) comes out of an assignment or appointment from God. This is critical and foundational to Christian leadership. When someone recruits you to a job that you are not called to, it's easy to throw in the towel when the going gets tough.

I think of some of the policemen in New Orleans who started handing in their badges in the midst of the flooding and looting after hurricane Katrina. I can understand why they'd want to quit under those horrific circumstances—I can't blame them, especially since it was just a $16,000 a year job. I'm guessing none of the officers who handed in their badges would have said they were "called" to their positions. Why? Because when you're called, you're willing to surrender, even your life.

This reminds me of an old story; maybe you've heard it: A pastor, a lawyer and an engineer were about to be guillotined. The pastor put his head on the block, they pulled the rope and nothing happened. So he said, "Praise God, I've been saved by divine intervention," so they let him go. The lawyer was then put on the block, and again the rope didn't release the blade, so he said, "You can't try executing me a second time for the same crime," and he too was set free. The engineer's turn was next, so they shoved his head into the guillotine. He looked up at the release mechanism and said, "Hold on a second…I see your problem." That's making a surrender for your calling!

> ## Caution
>
> Jesus warned his followers to count the cost of being his disciple. As a Christian leader, it's crucial to recognize Satan's strategy to weaken the church by attacking its leaders. The strategy is decapitation. Remove leadership, and affect the whole organization.

Being a small group leader is more than a commitment. Commitments are overrun by other commitments…especially in our culture today. I remember well the line from the England Dan and John Ford Coley song: "Well it's sad to belong to someone else when the right one comes along." Unfortunately that attitude is prevalent in today's world and in the church.

A commitment takes *dedication*. But a calling takes *surrender*. That reminds me of another song, one of my favorites: "I will abandon it all for the sake of the call." If God has called you to be a small group leader, say, *Yes, God. I will abandon it all for the sake of your call. I surrender.*

REMEMBER: A commitment takes dedication. But a calling takes *surrender*.

That may not be easy. I remember when God called me and my wife to move to

Idaho. Several relatives and friends could not comprehend how we could make the move. How could we move our kids away from their grandparents, aunts, uncles, and cousins, they asked. I admit it wasn't easy. It was tough. But we knew and tried to explain to others that God had called us to go. We felt a little like Abraham who "obeyed and went," even though he did not know where he was going. Our calling by God trumped over any possible circumstances, consequences, or even personal feelings.

UNEXPECTED CALLS

God often assigns leadership positions to people we might not expect. He chose the shepherd boy, David, over his older, bigger, and more skilled brothers. He chose Jonah even though he kept running away and hiding. He chose some ordinary and uneducated fishermen, tax collectors, and other assorted riffraff over the elite, educated Pharisees. Why? Because "the Lord does not look at the things man looks at. Man looks at the outward appearance, but the Lord looks at the heart" (1 Samuel 16:7). From those he chose in Scripture, I think one of the main attributes God looks at is a heart surrendered to him.

When God calls you, he is looking for a surrendered heart.

When Jesus called some fishermen, they surrendered their business, families, identities (as fishermen), and who knows what else to follow him. When Jesus called, Matthew surrendered his career. When Jesus called, Saul he surrendered his religion, his reputation, and his retinal orientation. When he calls you, he is also looking for a surrendered heart.

YOU'RE GIFTED!

Spiritual leadership is a gift. You don't earn it. You can't achieve it. You don't really even deserve it. If you grab leadership, it's not a gift. You just accept it with a surrendered heart. It's a gift of God's grace in your life.

I've heard people say that only about 5-10 percent of the people in any given church have the spiritual gift of leadership. I wonder where they got that statistic from. It's not in the Bible! I believe lots of God's people can be servant-leaders. And, by the way, that's the only kind of spiritual leaders the Bible talks about.

God has and will give you the gift to lead as you need it. Like Moses, he'll put you into some situations where you'll need to provide leadership, and you may not think you have what it takes to do it, but if he puts you in that situation, he'll also give you everything you need to carry out his will (see Exodus 4). He'll give it to you as a gift of his grace.

> "By God's special favor and mighty power, I have been given the wonderful privilege of serving him by spreading this Good News. Just think! Though I did nothing to deserve it, and though I am the least deserving Christian there is, I was chosen for this special joy of telling the Gentiles about the endless treasures available to them in Christ."
>
> —Ephesians 3:7, NLT

SURRENDER YOUR LEADERSHIP

Years ago, as a new Christian, I was thrust into ministry quickly. At the time I did not understand surrender, so I tried to lead by my own power. I learned very quickly about God's power being made perfect in my weakness (2 Corinthians 12:9). I got really good at making God's power perfect! He used me even though I had no idea what I was doing most of the time. But I also made lots of mistakes.

GET OUT OF THE WAY SO GOD CAN GET TO WORK

I was sharing my faith—or trying to—with one couple in our apartment building. I spent months using every tactic I had learned, and then some...with no results. Finally, my wife told me to back off. I couldn't believe it! *What a backslider!* I was fulfilling the Great Commission. I had married a heretic! Then she told me that perhaps I needed to leave room for the Holy Spirit to work in their lives. She was right, of course. I receded and eventually the couple came to Christ, about a year after we moved from the building.

In my ministry today, I've been in lots of overwhelming situations. I've talked on the phone with people threatening suicide. I've walked into hospital rooms of dying patients whose families needed comfort. I've entered homes where men had died in their prime. In one case—and I wasn't ready for this—the man's body was still on the floor in the living room when I walked in.

Had I faced the same situations years ago, I may have done more damage than good by trying to minister in my own power. Over the last several years, however, I've been learning more about surrender—yielding the situation completely to God. Now, as soon as I get a phone call or enter into a situation, the first thing I do is surrender the situation to God. I say to him something like:

"For I am overwhelmed, and you alone know the way I should turn."

—Psalm 143:3

God, you know I don't have whatever's needed to minister to this family. I don't have the right words, and I'm not sure how to handle this. I've got nothing! But I know that you do have all the right words and you do know what is needed. So I'm once again surrendering myself to you. Use me any way you want. If they need words, speak the words through my voice. If they just need someone to be there, help me to be quiet and to just be there with them through this. If they need some counsel, give me the words to say at the right time. Whatever their need, God, you know what it is, so use me any way you want. I'm all yours.

I am still always amazed at what happens. God does his work, whether I understand it or not. There's nothing really magical or mystical about it, but I know God has used my weakness to demonstrate his power. One family sent me a card that thanked me for how I ministered to them through my caring attitude, my words, and even my humor. When I received the letter I chuckled.

"I am a little pencil in the hand of a writing God who is sending a love letter to the world."
—Mother Teresa

When you surrender your leadership to God, allowing him to use you any way he wants to, you will minister in ways you thought you never could. In fact, you will learn, as I have, that it's not about what you do at all.

WHAT SURRENDER REQUIRES

To learn to surrender, you first need to grow in some other biblical characteristics. The best small group leader ever illustrated all these character traits perfectly:

REMEMBER:
God uses our weaknesses to demonstrate his power.

1. **Humility**—It all begins here. Surrender demands a humble heart. Jesus humbled himself when he "made himself nothing" and left Heaven to become human (Philippians 2:7, 8). Humility is the opposite of selfish ambition and vain conceit (v. 3).

2. **Authenticity**—A humble person can be who he or she really is without pretenses. Even though he was, by his very nature, God (v. 6), he came and lived as a man (v. 8). He never denied either part of his identity. He knew and lived who he was.

3. **Vulnerability**—An authentic person can be open and honest with others; he has nothing to hide.

4. **Submission/Obedience**—A surrendered heart means you are submissive to authority. Jesus obeyed his Father in everything, even death (v. 8).

5. **Integrity**—All of these characteristics lead to integrity— uncompromising adherence to truth. Jesus was the model of integrity. He was the truth (John 14:6). Integrity elicits trust, a vital characteristic of a small group leader.

WHAT SURRENDER PRODUCES

A surrendered leader is one who is connected to the Vine. You are dependent on the Vine. You will produce much fruit (John 15:5). You naturally put the interests of others before your own by:

LISTENING TO THEM

SERVING THEM

LOVING THEM

PRAYING FOR THEM

These are some of the attributes of an effective leader, but there is one more that needs a little more discussion.

SURRENDER PROPELS GROUP GROWTH

God has called you to help bring about spiritual growth in people's lives. But how does that happen, exactly? What's your role?

Imagine you are the captain of a sailboat. How do you make the vessel move forward toward your destination? The wind and only the wind supplies the power necessary for movement. If the wind is not blowing, you might as well forget raising the sails. How about having all the people on the boat blow as hard as they can into the sails? No, that won't work either. No matter how much effort you expend—no matter how much you huff and puff—you cannot move the ship forward. You cannot create wind.

So what do you do? You wait for the wind and then raise the sails to catch it. What happens if you do not raise the sails? Nothing. The power is accessible, but you must do your part in the partnership—raise the sails. The wind can propel you forward only when you are engaged in it. Sailing is a partnership between man and nature.

Spiritual growth is a collaborative effort between you and God. You cannot do it without God. He has ordained not to do it without you. The term for *Spirit* is the same as that for *wind* in both the Old and New Testaments. The

Holy Spirit is the wind that provides the driving force of all spiritual growth. You cannot bring about spiritual growth in your own life or the lives of those you lead.

Neither are you a passive bystander. As the Holy Spirit moves, you must become engaged in that driving force. As a small group leader you have at least four vital sail-raising responsibilities:

1. **Pray for the members of your group. That's your first and most important job.**

2. **Be an example to the flock. Let them see spiritual growth happening in your own life by being involved in the spiritual disciplines of worship, Bible reading, prayer, and others.**

3. **Involve the group every week in practices such as meeting in authentic community, studying and applying God's Word together, teaching and admonishing one another, praying together, serving together, even confessing your sins to each other.**

4. **Shepherd your members outside of group meeting times. Be prepared to mentor them in areas where they need to grow, as God leads you.**

I'll tell you how to raise that last sail in much more detail in the next chapter.

NOW WHAT?

✔ **What specifically do you need to surrender to God right now?**

✔ **Where do you need to *stop* leading so that the Holy Spirit can lead?**

✔ **What can you do to raise the sails to engage in what God wants to do through you?**

---

[1] Bill Thrall, Bruce McNicol, and Ken McElrath, *The Ascent of a Leader* (San Francisco: Jossey-Bass Publishers, 1999), 81.

[2] John Fischer, "Under New Ownership," *The Purpose Driven Daily Devotional*, August 17, 2005. http://www.purposedrivenlife.com.

[3] Henry and Richard Blackaby, *Spiritual Leadership* (Nashville: Broadman & Holman Publishers, 2001), 43.

[4] Bill Bright, "Would You Like to Know God Personally?" (Campus Crusade for Christ).

Shepherd 4

> **Shepherd:**
> *A person who protects, guides, or watches over a person or group of people; the Shepherd, Jesus Christ (Dictionary.com).*

In the last two chapters, I've shown you the foundational heart attitudes for small group leadership. You cannot shepherd people like the best small group leader ever unless you are seeking and surrendering.

God's Word is rich in its discussion about shepherding. Moses, David, and Amos served as shepherds, and all were influenced greatly by that role in their leadership. *Shepherd* is applied in Scripture to God, Jesus, kings and other leaders of the people, local church leaders, and ministers (not necessarily paid staff ministers).

For you to fully understand your calling as your group's shepherd, I need to distinguish between your role as a shepherd of the flock under your care and Jesus' role as the Chief Shepherd.

DUTIES OF THE SHEPHERD

* to feed the sheep even if he has to gather them in his arms to carry them to the pasture
* to guide the sheep to the pasture and away from the rough places and precipices
* to seek and save sheep who get lost
* to protect the sheep; he is even willing to sacrifice his life for the sheep
* to restore sheep who go astray and return
* to reward the sheep for obedience and faithfulness
* to keep the sheep separate from the goats

—*Practical Word Studies in the New Testament*

ONE SHEPHERD

I'm using the word *shepherd* in this book to describe your role as a small group leader. But that's actually not quite right. Let me explain:

▶▶ *God's church has lots of sheep, but only one true shepherd.*

It is essential for you to understand that you are not the real shepherd, the chief shepherd. That role belongs exclusively to Jesus.

That God is our only shepherd is a theme throughout Scripture. King David declared it centuries earlier: "The Lord is my shepherd" (Psalm 23:1). His son Solomon also confirmed this: "The words of the wise prod us to live well. They're like nails hammered home, holding life together. They are given by God, the one Shepherd" (Ecclesiastes 12:11, *The Message*). The Lord is our only source of wisdom and our one true shepherd.

> **THE BEST SMALL GROUP LEADER EVER SAID...**
>
> *"I am the good shepherd. I know my sheep, and my sheep know me. ... I have other sheep that are not of this sheep pen. I must bring them also. They too will listen to my voice, and there will be one flock and one shepherd."*
> —John 10:14-16 (my emphasis)

> "The Great Shepherd is one of the thrusts of Biblical scripture. This illustration encompasses many ideas, including God's care for his people, His discipline to correct the wandering sheep, as well as the tendency of humans to put themselves into danger's way and their inability to guide and take care of themselves apart from the direct power and leading of God."
> —Wikipedia.org

The *New Living Translation* renders "chief shepherd" in 1 Peter 5 as "head shepherd." Just as Jesus is the head of the body of Christ (Ephesians 4:15; Colossians 1:18), he is the head shepherd. He is the real leader of "your" group.

Jesus is the head shepherd of the group. Yet God designed his church as a partnership with human beings. You are called to represent him, carry out his plans, fulfill his commission, and perform the ministry he gives you to do. He is the king; you are his ambassador. He is the owner of the group; you are his steward. He is the chief shepherd; you are his "subordinate shepherd."

JESUS' ROLE AS THE CHIEF SHEPHERD	YOUR ROLE AS A SUBORDINATE SHEPHERD
• Knows his sheep and makes it possible for the sheep to know him • Lays down his life for the sheep • Calls the sheep by name • Seeks after the lost sheep and draws them to himself • Provides eternal life and abundant life	• Follow the Chief Shepherd • Model following the Chief Shepherd • Help the sheep under your care to hear and respond to the Chief Shepherd's voice • Guide the sheep under your care to follow the Good Shepherd and reach out to sheep without a shepherd • Encourage the sheep to live the abundant life

After Jesus rose from the dead, he called Peter as one of his first subordinate shepherds: "Feed my lambs...take care of my sheep...feed my sheep" (John 21:15-17). Whose lambs? Whose sheep? Not Peter's. Not yours. Not your senior minister's. Jesus'!

WiSe WorDs

JESUS IS...

➤ **The Good Shepherd (John 10:11,15)**

➤ **The Great Shepherd (Hebrews 13:20, 21)**

➤ **The Shepherd and Guardian of Our Souls (1 Peter 2:25)**

➤ **The Chief Shepherd (1 Peter 5:4)**

I'll continue to use the term *shepherd* to describe your role (and *subordinate shepherd* when needed for clarity). Just remember that you shepherd under the Chief Shepherd's authority—which is why the previous chapter about surrender is so vital. You shepherd the group as an act of stewardship. The group is not yours, but God has *entrusted* you with them for now to care for and manage well. I'll discuss stewardship of the group in more detail in Chapter 7.

As you lead the group, remember, you are one of the sheep. Jesus is your shepherd. You are not above the other sheep, so you have no right to lord it over them, because you are not the Lord either. Jesus has called you as his representative and as a good steward to care for the fellow sheep he's temporarily entrusted to you. So take your responsibility seriously.

SUBORDINATE SHEPHERDS

"I believe a Life Group Leader is one of the most significant ministry opportunities we offer at Northeast. Rarely does a person have the opportunity to impact the life of a fellow believer the way a Life Group Leader can." (Steve Idle, teaching pastor, Northeast Christian Church, Louisville, Kentucky. We call our small groups "Life Groups" at Northeast.)

That's a great summary of the identity, influence, and importance of shepherd-leaders in God's church. Some churches ask their small group leaders to be merely discussion facilitators or hosts. Those roles are significant in the group, but the leader is called to be a shepherd to the sheep.

As a small group leader, you are given the authority and responsibility to carry out the pastoral ministry of the church in your group. That's a big assignment, but you're not alone!

The best small group leader ever modeled

Jesus used the imagery of shepherds and sheep as a parable or metaphor. Parables usually have one simple, straightforward meaning from which we can learn. But be careful not to read too much into them or stretch them beyond the intended application. For instance, in the real world of real sheepfolds and shepherds, sheep are not entrusted to lead other sheep or called as subordinate shepherds. But in the spiritual world, this is the case. We are more than just dumb sheep. Jesus calls each of us as his partners in his mission.

shepherding for the members of his group and us. He illustrated how vitally important the role of a shepherd is as he walked among the throngs of people and "had compassion on them, because they were harassed and helpless, like sheep without a shepherd" (Matthew 9:36). That these people were aimlessly wandering through life with no one to guide, care for, feed, and protect them broke Jesus' heart. So take your assignment of shepherding very seriously. You are an answer to his prayer for more workers to bring in the harvest (vv. 37, 38).

Your responsibility as a small group leader is primarily to shepherd the sheep that God puts into your care and to go out and bring more sheep into the fold. So…

Do *not* view yourself merely as a Bible study teacher or the equivalent of a Sunday school teacher who presents lessons to the group.

Do *not* limit your role to that of a meeting facilitator who plans and conducts discussions.

Do *not* think of yourself only as a disc-jockey, whose job is to put the DVD in the player and push *play*.

Small group pioneer Ralph Neighbour put it this way:

The Shepherd never says, "I will tend the flock on Wednesday evenings from 7:00 to 9:30 p.m." No! The Shepherd lives with the flock, sleeps in the fields with the flock, goes into treacherous situations to find a lost sheep, and carries the lambs in his arms. The Shepherd is the first one to go into the "valley of the shadow of death" to lead sheep to "green pastures."[1]

THE PSALM OF THE NO-GOOD SHEPHERD

This leader is the shepherd
I do not want.
He maketh me sit down on green love seats;
he leadeth me to meetings.
He ignoreth my soul.
He leadeth me to complete my homework assignment—
It taketh three hours, for heaven's sake.
Yea, though I walk through the valley of downsizing
and debt, you are not with me.
Your wife and the church staff; they run from me.
You preparest a table of fattening foods before me.
You are my enemies.
My blood's about to boil;
My disappointment overflows.
Surely your incessant e-mails will follow me all the days of my life;
And I shall dwell in this lousy group forever!

The Bible is not silent about your role as a small group shepherd. Look at the following scriptural guidelines:

THE DIFFERENCE BETWEEN A SHEPHERD AND A HIRED HAND

	A SHEPHERD...	A HIRED HAND...
JOHN 10:1-16	Cares to the point of sacrifice	Quits when the going is tough
	Knows sheep personally	Knows the sheep as a flock
	Intimate relationship with God	Is in it for personal advancement
	Heart for the sheep	Just doing the job

I'm A Leader... Now What? **47**

Acts 20:28:

"Keep watch over yourselves and all the flock of which the Holy Spirit has made you overseers. Be shepherds of the church of God, which he bought with his own blood."

Proverbs 27:23:

"Be sure you know the condition of your flocks, give careful attention to your herds."

Ezekiel 34:1-6:
Roles:

* To strengthen the weak
* To heal the sick
* To bind up the injured
* To bring back the strays and seek the lost
* To lead gently and not harshly

As mentioned earlier, you can divide your shepherding role into three vital relationships: connecting your group into authentic community with one another, discipling them to grow in their relationships with God, and encouraging them to make an impact by serving others. I'll address each of these throughout the rest of this chapter.

THREE RELATIONSHIPS OF SHEPHERDING

Connecting your group into authentic community with one another

Discipling them to grow in their relationships with God

Encouraging them to make an impact serving others

#1: GUIDE THEM TO AUTHENTIC COMMUNITY

One of the first things you do as a leader is to build relationships with the members of the group. This should begin way before the first meeting.

Finding Your Group

If you are just getting started and do not have group members yet, start with prayer. Ask God to show you exactly who he wants in your group. Then keep your eyes open to whom he will send. It's highly likely—but not absolute—that these will be people already in your circle, people you already know. They may be friends, neighbors, coworkers, people you serve with or otherwise know from church, for instance.

To keep your eyes open for whom God sends, ask him for the spiritual eyes to see. In John 1:47-49, when Jesus saw Nathanael (who would be one of Jesus' small group members) approaching him, he said, "Here is a true Israelite, in whom there is nothing false." This surprised Nathanael. "How do you know me?" he asked. Jesus answered, "I saw you while you were still under the fig tree before Philip called you." How did Jesus "see" Nathanael, whom he had never met? He had been praying that the Father would make known to him those whom the Father was going to give him out of the world (John 17:6).

I am in the midst of starting a new "turbo group." When I first began planning it, I knew that the selection of this group would be critical to the future of our small group ministry. So I decided not to "recruit" the group or even list names of those I thought should be in the group. Instead, I prayed every day that God would bring them. Because I believe these will be future leaders in our small groups ministry, I did what the best small group leader ever said to do: "Ask the Lord of the harvest, therefore, to send out workers into his harvest field" (Matthew 9:38). I also asked for God to give me the eyes to see them when they came.

Definitions

Turbo Group:

A small group that lasts about three to twenty-four months in which every member is a leader-in-training and will begin a new group at the conclusion of the group.

Larry walked in the front door of our office building one day and asked to see the small group minister. I reluctantly set aside my turbo group planning and went out to meet him, a bit dismayed by the unannounced intrusion into my work. Larry and his wife Glenda had been led to Christ by Ralph Neighbour, one of the pioneers of small group ministry. They had spent years in ministry themselves, and had recently moved to Louisville, looking for a church where they could be involved. Larry wanted to get back to his first love of small groups.

I had known Chris and Tiffany for several years. Chris works on our backstage crew and has a huge servant's heart. One Sunday morning before the service I saw Chris standing around. It seemed odd to me that he apparently had nothing to do. Something inside me told me to go over and talk to him. I obeyed, but had no idea why. On my walk over, God told me—and it was extremely clear—to ask Chris to be in the group. I stopped for a moment in the middle of our lobby. Chris is a successful home builder in our area, but I had not yet considered him as a potential small group leader. Finally I obeyed, told Chris about the group, and invited him. I expected him to say he'd have to think about it, but he immediately said, "Yeah! I'm in!"

The stories about how each of the other members came and how I knew them are also unique and amazing. They are each testimonies to the fact that God really is the Chief Shepherd.

Getting Started

As you begin, always start with a core group. One of the essential values of leading a small group is *don't start alone!* Meet together over meals, building your team by getting to know one another. Begin planning the group together, getting ownership and involvement. Divide group tasks based on individuals' spiritual gifts and interests. Then, as a team, begin inviting others to your new group. (I'll discuss more about building a team with your group in Chapter 6, "Share.")

#2: ESTABLISH RELATIONSHIPS

One of your primary tasks—if you can call it that—is to build relationships with group members. By starting with a core team, you have already begun. Now, as a team, each of you focuses on building relationships with other participants outside of meeting times.

God created people with a high need for real relationships. I read about a man who walked into a convenience store, threatened the clerk with a knife, and demanded cash. When she gave him the money, he thanked her, walked out and proceeded to sit down on the curb in front of the store. When police arrived, he jumped up and announced that he was the man they were looking for. The baffled police put him in cuffs and took him in.

At the trial, he gave his reason for robbing the store and immediately giving himself up. He had only recently been released from jail, missed his cell mates, and wanted to return to jail so he could be with them. He got his wish. That's the power of community. Some people will do just about anything for it.

Paul and Silas could have related to this story:

> **They were severely beaten, and then they were thrown into prison. The jailer was ordered to make sure they didn't escape. So he took no chances but put them into the inner dungeon and clamped their feet in the stocks. Around midnight, Paul and Silas were praying and singing hymns to God, and the other prisoners were listening (Acts 16:23-25, *NLT*).**

You have probably figured out by now that the power of community increases the more people are together. Once a week or every other week meetings do not bring the kind of close-knit community you often see in the New Testament. But how do you make this happen, short of incarcerating your whole group? It takes time together, spontaneous and planned. It may take proximity, meeting with the people where you live

The power of community increases the more people are together.

or work, for instance. It may take forming your group around people who have things in common. Instead of trying to find another brand-new group of friends, ask yourself, *Who is already in my life?*

A big part of your role as a leader is to (1) live this kind of interdependent life yourself and (2) to do everything you can to help develop this kind of authentic, groundbreaking community! As a shepherd, what do you do to make this happen?

WiSe WoRds

"Every day they continued to meet together" (Acts 2:46).

"Encourage one another daily" (Hebrews 3:13).

"Let us not give up meeting together, as some are in the habit of doing, but let us encourage one another" (Hebrews 10:25).

✔ *Pray regularly* for and with the members of your group.

✔ *Keep in touch* between meetings. Call, e-mail, visit.

✔ *Accept everyone,* regardless of personality differences.

"[Here's] a deep theological truth: Everybody's weird. Every one of us—all we like sheep—have habits we can't control, past deeds we can't undo, flaws we can't correct." [2]

—John Ortberg, *Everybody's Normal Till You Get to Know Them*

✔ *Deal with conflicts up front.* Don't try to wish them away or pretend they aren't there. For more help on this subject, see Pat Sikora's HELP! Guide: *Why Didn't You Warn Me?*

✔ *Stay positive.* Group members sometimes tend to become negative—about other people, the church, you name it. Turn the tide as soon as you can. It seems like a lot of people complain and gossip, but very few people want to be in a negative group.

✔ *Focus on people,* not the program. As Ralph Neighbor says, "The people in your group are the agenda!" [3]

Community is the environment in which everything else happens in a small group. It is the soil in which people grow spiritually.

#3: GUIDE THEM TO GROW SPIRITUALLY

As a small group shepherd you are in the most strategic position in the church to effect real, lasting life change and spiritual growth. The church's best method for caring, shepherding, loving, and growing people is you!

You may have heard assertions like this before, and while they are true, you may be asking how you are supposed to make it happen.

First, as a shepherd leader, be concerned for where people are in their spiritual journeys.

You need to know where people are in order to shepherd them to where they ought to be. Accept group members where they are on their spiritual journeys. Treat each person with grace, not judgment. At the same time, help group members grow. Encourage. Spur each other on. Teach and admonish one another in all wisdom.

Second, model a disciple's lifestyle.

Spiritual growth must be happening in your life as the leader. You are a model for what life change looks like to others.

Third, keep providing the context.

Continue to draw the group into increasing levels of authentic community. Don't give up meeting together, and people will grow.

Fourth, assess where group members are on their spiritual journeys.

A number of assessments are available, including:

- "The Christian Life Profile," which assesses spiritual growth along thirty core competencies (by Randy Frazee; http://www.zondervan.com)

- "Growth Finder" an online discipleship assessment (http://www. churchteams.com/GrowthFinder.asp)

- "Purpose Driven Spiritual Health Assessment and Spiritual Health Planner" (http://www.purposedriven.com)

These tools can help group members know where they are spiritually, and will help you develop a strategy for helping them grow.

Fifth, provide a process for growth to happen.

Do application-oriented Bible study as a group. Don't just study the Bible. Do what it says! What do you study? The answer comes from knowing your group and what they need most to grow. Ask a small group coach or minister from your church for more help.

DID YOU KNOW ...

"In the spiritual care of God's children, the feeding of the flock from the Word of God is the constant and regular necessity; it is to have the foremost place. The tending (which includes this) consists of other acts, of discipline, authority, restoration, material assistance of individuals, but they are incidental in comparison with the feeding."[4]

—*Expository Dictionary of New Testament Words*

Sixth, be a spiritual parent to the group.

Mentor some members one-on-one. Ask group members who are relatively strong in one spiritual area to disciple a person who would like to grow in the same area. This gets everyone involved in the spiritual growth process.

Spiritual parenting means that you don't see all group members the same. You shepherd them individually, because they are at different places in their spiritual journeys. Some are infants, some are adolescents or teens, while others are maturing adults.

The apostle John wrote in 1 John 2:12-14:

I write to you, dear children, because your sins have been forgiven on account of his name. I write to you, fathers, because you have known him who is from the beginning. I write to you, young men, because you have overcome the evil one. I write to you, dear children, because you have known the Father. I write to you, fathers, because you have known him who is from the beginning. I write to you, young men, because you are strong, and the word of God lives in you, and you have overcome the evil one.

John had learned from *his* small group leader how to shepherd the sheep individually.

> **He tends his flock like a shepherd:**
> **He gathers the lambs in his arms**
> **and carries them close to his heart;**
> **he gently leads those that have young.**
> —Isaiah 40:11

Finally, develop leaders.

I'll discuss this more in Chapter 6, but it's important to mention here because it is a part of every group member's spiritual growth process. Continually developing and deploying new leaders is essential for what comes next.

GUIDE THEM TO WHERE THE CHIEF SHEPHERD WANTS THEM TO GO

Here's a fact borne by years of experience: Group members do not always want to go where they need to go. They resist growing spiritually, being open to new people, stepping out to serve others, stepping up to become leaders, and sending out members to birth new groups. Group member sometimes prefer comfort to counting the cost.

"A leader is a person you will follow to a place you wouldn't go by yourself." [5]
—**Joel Barker**

From what I understand, sheep can be pretty stubborn animals. My black lab can be pretty dogged as well. She loves to go on car rides, so, if we're not careful, she'll jump in the van with the family even when she's not invited. She's usually a very good, obedient dog, but not when it comes to getting her out of that van!

I've had small group members who were the same way. Once you get them into a group, they never want to leave! Jesus says, *Go* and make disciples, but it does not matter. All they want to do is *stay* and make cookies!

Your role as a small group subordinate shepherd is to take group members to the places the Chief Shepherd commands. That may not always be easy and definitely not comfortable, but it's one of your most important responsibilities. Your job is to listen to the Chief Shepherd's voice closely, every day. Read his Word regularly. Stay involved in learning and growing yourself. Continue to be equipped for your role as a small group leader. Go to every training event and read every book you can.

TRY THIS!

For more great training, go to The Small Group Network web site at http://smallgroups.com. See the last page of this book for a free trial-membership coupon. The site includes e-Training modules that include audio and visual effects to make learning experiential and fun.

I've seen many groups—and even entire churches—cow-tow to members who prefer comfort rather than following God's commands. I've heard small group ministers say something like, "Well, our members won't open up their groups to new members or send out members to start groups, so we've changed our methodology to make it work with what we can reasonably expect our groups to do."

May I implore you? Don't do this! Hold high the values that the greatest small group leader ever gave us. His commission is to go and make disciples…so go and make disciples! And don't ever forget that your sheep have an enemy out there who is ready to deceive, diminish, and even devour them. As your group is going into the world, your job is to help guard them against attacks. Of course you can't do this on your own, but only by God's mighty power. The shepherd David reported that "When a lion or a bear came and carried off a sheep from the flock, I went after it, struck it and rescued the sheep from its mouth. When it turned on me, I seized it by its hair, struck it and killed it" (I Samuel 17:34, 35). That's impressive shepherding! But look at how he did it; he said it was the Lord "who delivered me from the paw of the lion and the paw of the bear" (v. 37).

"Be self-controlled and alert. Your enemy the devil prowls around like a roaring lion looking for someone to devour."

—1 Peter 5:8

You will not be fighting lions and bears (oh my)! But you are on a dangerous, crucial mission. The last thing the enemy wants is for your group to grow spiritually. He knows that Christians who are transformed into Christ's likeness (2 Corinthians 3:18) become dangerous to his agenda. So he will put up a fight, and he'll start with you.

Perhaps you've never considered leading your small group as doing spiritual battle, but it is a more real and critical fight than any battle ever fought in this physical world. So start your preparation on your knees. Pray through Ephesians 6:10-20. Pray specifically for each member of your group. Surrender yourself to God. Commit your plans to him. Submit to his authority and power. Acknowledge that it is his group, not yours. Ask him for his protection as you lead your group where the Chief Shepherd is calling you to go.

> "The duty of shepherds was to keep their flock intact and protect it from predators, such as wolves and bears. The shepherd was also to supervise the migration of the flock."
> —Wikipedia.org

The greatest small group leader ever said, "I'm here to invite outsiders, not coddle insiders" (Matthew 9:13, *The Message*). That's what he's put you here for, too. I'll talk more about it in Chapter 5.

NOW WHAT?

Take a moment right now to write down two specific things you will do differently to shepherd your group more like the Good Shepherd.

1 . _____

2 . _____

[1] Ralph W. Neighbour, Jr., *The Shepherd's Guidebook* rev. ed. (Houston, Texas: TOUCH Outreach Ministries, 1996), 34.

[2] John Ortberg, *Everybody's Normal Till You Get to Know Them* (Grand Rapids, Michigan: Zondervan, 2003), 18.

[3] Neighbour, 67.

[4] *Expository Dictionary of New Testament Words* (Old Tappan, New Jersey: Fleming H. Revell, 1966).

[5] from the Kent Crockett web site: http://www.kentcrockett.com/.

Serve 5

Serve:
to render assistance; be of use; help; to render active service to (a sovereign, commander, etc.); to render obedience or homage to (God, a sovereign, etc.) (Dictionary.com).

I'm a huge college basketball fan. During "March Madness" every year I am glued to the television, following all the tournaments with my boys. I love watching the games, of course, but I also like some of the commercials. In one, Coach K (Mike Krzyzewski, head coach of Duke, for non- basketball fans) made a fascinating comment: "I don't see myself as a basketball coach. I see myself as a leader who happens to coach basketball." That's interesting, but it's backwards for Christian leaders. Jesus calls us to see ourselves not so much as leaders but as servants who happen to lead.

Did you know that your very nature as a Christian is as a servant? When God bought you with Jesus' blood (Ephesians 1:7) and you surrendered your life to him, you became his servant. You *belong* to him (Romans 14:8). Jesus spent a lot of time trying to teach his small group this lesson. It took them a long time and a lot of bickering about who was greatest before they got it. In fact, it was not until after Jesus performed the ultimate act of service that they understood fully and began to live with servant attitudes.

THE BEST SMALL GROUP LEADER EVER SAID...

"For even the Son of Man did not come to be served, but to serve, and to give his life as a ransom for many."
—Mark 10:45

The apostles, especially Paul, also spent a lot of time and effort trying to convince believers of their identity as God's servants—not servants of other things:

PASSAGE	SCRIPTURE (NLT)	SERVE GOD, NOT...
MATTHEW 6:24	No one can serve two masters. For you will hate one and love the other, or be devoted to one and despise the other. You cannot serve both God and money.	MONEY
ROMANS 6:6	Our old sinful selves were crucified with Christ so that sin might lose its power in our lives. We are no longer slaves to sin.	SIN
ROMANS 7:6	Now we can really serve God, not in the old way by obeying the letter of the law, but in the new way, by the Spirit.	THE LAW
ROMANS 16:18	Such people are not serving Christ our Lord; they are serving their own personal interests.	YOURSELF
GALATIANS 4:8	Before you Gentiles knew God, you were slaves to so-called gods that do not even exist.	IDOLS
COLOSSIANS 3:23, 24	Work hard and cheerfully at whatever you do, as though you were working for the Lord rather than for people. Remember that the Lord will give you an inheritace as your reward, and the Master you are serving is Christ.	PEOPLE

Like the greatest leader ever, your spiritual nature is to be a servant (Philippians 2:7). And, like Jesus, your role as a leader is to model servanthood to others. So, "never be lacking in zeal, but keep your spiritual fervor, serving the Lord." Or as the *New Living Translation* put it, "serve the Lord enthusiastically." In our main passage from 1 Peter 5:2-4, Peter says we are to be "eager to serve." Eager and enthusiastic to serve—sounds like a paradox to me, but it is your call as a leader.

A SERVANT WHO LEADS

Your nature is to serve. God calls some servants to lead. It's never the other way around. If you can serve best by leading, and that is what God has called you to, then, by all means, lead with diligence! (Romans 12:8). But if you can serve better in some other fashion, or if someone else can lead better than you, or if God has not called you to lead, then serve in some other way—with diligence!

Caution

While your spiritual nature is to serve God, your human nature is to serve yourself and all kinds of other worldly things. Again, being a leader puts you square in the middle of a spiritual battle.

THE BEST SMALL GROUP LEADER EVER SAID...

"But among you, those who are the greatest should take the lowest rank, and the leader should be like a servant."

—Luke 22:26, *NLT*

How you approach your leadership—as a leader first or as a servant first—makes all the difference in the world. If you come at leadership as a leader first, you naturally try to control, make decisions, push your agenda, and give orders. If you come at leadership as a servant first, you build partnership and shared leadership. You develop a team. Leadership is not a power play or an ego-trip for you. You serve in this role because you are called to it, because people need a shepherd.

As a servant leader you will discover the need to fight the stature of the position. You live it with humility. Servant-leaders are often somewhat reluctant to lead, not because they don't think they can or doubt God's call, but because of the stature our society often assigns to leaders.

The Difference Between Leader-First and Servant-First Leadership[1]

LEADERS FIRST...	SERVANTS FIRST...
Naturally try to control, make decisions, and give orders	Assume leadership only if it is the best way to serve
Are "driven" to lead	Are "called" to lead
Are possessive about their leadership position; they think they "own" it	View leadership as an act of stewardship. If someone else is a better leader, they will partner with the person or find another place to serve.
Dislike feedback; it is threatening to their position	Like feedback; it helps them serve better

SERVE YOUR GROUP

While your nature is to serve God, not man, you are called as his subordinate shepherd to serve your group. That does not mean you put them first, before God, of course, but that you serve him by serving others.

Serve your group eagerly and enthusiastically. That takes *guts!*

GENUINELY: "Godliness leads to love for other Christians, and finally you will grow to have genuine love for everyone" (2 Peter 1:7, NLT).

> "Serve one another in love.
> —Galatians 5:13

UNCONDITIONALLY: God's love for us doesn't depend on what we do. It's unconditional. In biblical community we accept and love one another "as is" no matter what. They don't have to earn it.

TANGIBLY: In deed, not just words. "Think of ways to encourage one another to outbursts of love and good deeds" (Hebrews 10:24, NLT).

SACRIFICIALLY: Jesus said, "The greatest love is shown when people lay down their lives for their friends" (John 15:13, NLT).

How can you serve your group members "tangibly" (as well as genuinely, unconditionally, and sacrificially)? Here are a few ideas.

* **Make them dinner with all the trimmings**
* **Watch their kids and arrange for a night out on the town**
* **Take them to or pick them up from the airport, no matter what time it is**
* **Wash their vehicles**
* **Help with a household project**
* **Go to their kids' games and cheer**
* **Mow their lawn**

* Take an individual out for coffee and really listen
* Discover needs and meet them
* Ask them individually how you can pray for them—and then lift up their needs daily to God. Follow up by asking how things are going.

SERVE TOGETHER AS FRIENDS

After Jesus had spent nearly three years with his small group, he brought them together for a going away party. He was preparing to go away, but first he had to prepare them. He began by modeling for them how to serve one another by washing their feet. They shared a meal together, and he taught them some valuable lessons. Look at this passage:

> I'm no longer calling you servants because servants don't understand what their master is thinking and planning. No, I've named you friends because I've let you in on everything I've heard from the Father. You didn't choose me, remember; I chose you, and put you in the world to bear fruit, fruit that won't spoil. As fruit bearers, whatever you ask the Father in relation to me, he gives you. But remember the root command: Love one another (John 15:15-17, *The Message*).

I see several vital principles in this passage for any group:

1. *You serve as friends.* This may seem obvious, but it wasn't to Jesus' group. It must have been a big deal to them that Jesus called them his friends. He was their Rabbi—their teacher—and they were his disciples. Now he was saying, "I'm calling you my equals, *my friends*." They were in authentic community with one another. Even though Jesus really was their Lord and teacher, they were now all co-laborers in the Father's kingdom. They had been serving to-gether—side-by-side—for a couple years. Now Jesus wanted them to continue serving together as friends, knowing that he would continue to be with them in spirit.

Like that group, yours is a group of friends who are called to serve together. The Chief Shepherd is still here to guide you as you go into the world to serve.

2. *Remember that Jesus has chosen you, not the other way around.* The significance is that since he chose you, your responsibility is to do what he calls you to do. If you had chosen him, you might still think you're the one in charge, making all the decisions. Your nature as a Christian, is to serve God. He'll tell you what to do.

3. *He expects you to bear fruit.* He did not put you in the position of a small group leader to make sure the group is comfortable or just to do Bible study or just to have great fellowship. Your job is to bear fruit, fruit that will last.

Serve each other as friends—and don't forget to love one another.

4. *Don't forget—love one another!* That's the root command behind everything you do. Love each other in your group—and then extend that love to others outside your group. Let the love that God is pouring into you overflow into the lives of people around you. An overriding principle of this passage is this: The group does not exist primarily for its members; it exists for others.

One morning on the Christian radio station I usually listen to, a local preacher of the "church of the week" talked about the nature of the church. He said the teens from his congregation had written essays about the church, and all of them used the word *safe* in their descriptions. The preacher went on to say that this is an accurate portrayal of the church.

What do you think? Does *safe* describe the heart of Christ's church.

SAFE OR DANGEROUS?

Perhaps it is a matter of perspective. We do want people to feel like the church, and every small group within it, is a safe place. They will be accepted for who they are and where they are in life. They will not be attacked or abused.

On the other hand, God's Word portrays a church that is *dangerous*. It is in a war for the eternal destinies of humankind. It is a place of surrender and *sacrifice*. Peace comes in the midst of all this, as we put our trust in Christ. We are eternally safe because of his suffering, but we are on the front lines of a battle every day.

I think that is the gist of what Jesus was trying to teach his followers in Matthew 10, when he sent out the twelve to do ministry. He told them, "Do not suppose that I have come to bring peace to the earth. I did not come to bring peace, but a sword" (Matthew 10:34).

> ### THE BEST SMALL GROUP LEADER EVER SAID...
>
> "I have told you these things, so that in me you may have peace. In this world you will have trouble. But take heart! I have overcome the world."
>
> —John 16:33

That does not sound very safe to me! It has always fascinated me that in this passage Jesus says he did not come to bring peace, and yet he is the Prince of Peace. He said, "Peace I leave with you; my peace I give you. I do not give to you as the world gives. Do not let your hearts be troubled and do not be afraid" (John 14:27).

Perhaps that last verse holds the secret for small groups. The world defines peace as safety from trouble, but Christians know that in this world there will be trouble. Jesus has overcome the world, however. While difficulties and hardships will come, we do not have to let our hearts be troubled. As Christians, we do not need to seek safety and comfort. That is not the purpose of Christian small groups. We seek the mind of Christ—his purpose, will, and peace in the midst of whatever may come our way.

> ### THE BEST SMALL GROUP LEADER EVER SAID...
>
> "But seek first his kingdom and his righteousness, and all these things will be given to you as well."
>
> —Matthew 6:33

What You Can Do

One of your responsibilities as a small group leader is to keep a compelling vision in front of the group. Remind and encourage members that when you are involved in Jesus' mission and ministry, you will face trouble along the way. Ministry is not safe, but Jesus will provide his peace, comfort, and eternal safety as you carry out his commission. Here are five things you can do as a leader:

* **Remind group members frequently of your mission and group purposes. Use God's Word to teach the group about God's calling on the lives of Christians.**

* **Pray together with the same kind of power and vision with which the early church prayed (e.g. Acts 4:23-31).**

* **Build a community that cares deeply for one another: "All the believers were one in heart and mind. No one claimed that any of his possessions was his own, but they shared everything they had" (Acts 4:32).**

* **Equip group members for acts of service. Ephesians 4:11-13 was not written just for paid church staff members. It's written to you as a leader and shepherd as well. It calls you to "prepare God's people for works of service."**

* **Build a community that boldly reaches out to the world. "With great power the apostles continued to testify to the resurrection of the Lord Jesus, and much grace was upon them all" (Acts 4:33). Find ways to lovingly serve your community.**

Getting out of your recliners and loveseats and into the world may be a different paradigm for your group. It may scare some. It may sound terribly dangerous. Some group members may waver or even fight you on this. As a leader, stand firm. Have compassion for your group and those who have no Shepherd.

Over the last five years Northeast Christian Church has built a culture of serving our community. We do that serving primarily through our small groups. It's much better to serve together than alone. Serving also assures that our groups are not becoming ingrown cliques.

> **THE BEST SMALL GROUP LEADER EVER SAID...**
>
> "You're here to be light, bringing out the God-colors in the world. God is not a secret to be kept. We're going public with this, as public as a city on a hill. If I make you lightbearers, you don't think I'm going to hide you under a bucket, do you? I'm putting you on a light stand."
>
> —Matthew 5:14, 15,
> *The Message*

Your church and community have tons of opportunities to serve. First, you can serve together inside the church. Here are a few ideas that you could do together as a group. Ask around for more:

- ✔ **Campus cleanup or landscaping**
- ✔ **Take communion to shut-ins**
- ✔ **Work in the nursery or other department together (you may need to be approved and background checked first. If you do, volunteer to pay for the background check)**
- ✔ **Greet or usher**
- ✔ **Get a bunch of umbrellas and, on rainy days, walk people in from their cars**

Some of these you could do on a rotating basis, say the first Sunday of every month. Perhaps you could work with other groups to fill in all the Sundays!

You can also do externally focused ministry. Our groups regularly serve together in a variety of places throughout our community. We encourage our groups to eventually adopt a ministry as their "community cause." That is, they run point on it, planning and performing the ministry tasks together. In some cases they have joined together with an existing ministry to regularly help them out. In other cases, our groups have formed their own ministries and community causes. One group adopted a military helicopter pilot in Iraq. They regularly help the family and send care packages to the soldier. They have even joined the pilot in ministering to the children of Iraq by sending candy the helicopters drop as "candy bombs" to the children. The candy bombs help the children to not be afraid of the U.S., helicopters. This group's ministry to one family is having an impact in the world!

FOOD FOR THOUGHT

One church group prepares peanut-butter-and-jelly sandwiches and puts them in sacks with apples and other snacks. They deliver the lunches to many homeless people in downtown Louisville, Kentucky.

Another group prepares peanut-butter-and-jelly sandwiches and puts them in sacks with apples and other snacks. They deliver the lunches to many homeless people in downtown Louisville. Another group is planning to open a crisis pregnancy center in a community near our church. I had encouraged our groups to make "God-sized plans" for the next year (I'll discuss this more a little later). That is definitely God-sized for one small group!

These groups are not ordinary, safe, and comfortable. They are making big impact for Christ in our community. When your group moves out of the safe and comfortable and serves your community, you model authentic, profoundly powerful community to the world.

GO AND TELL TOGETHER

The best small group leader ever asked a philosophical question: "Who needs a doctor: the healthy or the sick?" The answer seems obvious, but the implication to your small group is more profound. Jesus then revealed his life mission: "I'm here inviting outsiders, not insiders—an invitation to a changed life, changed inside and out" (Luke 5:31, 32, *The Message*). Matthew's gospel says it slightly differently: "I'm here to invite outsiders, not coddle insiders" (Matthew 9:13).

Your small group exists for the same purpose: to invite outsiders, not coddle insiders! Your group is a community with a cause.

THE BEST SMALL GROUP LEADER EVER SAID...

"For the Son of Man came to seek and to save what was lost."
—Luke 19:10

Community-Based Invitations

The apostle John made a riveting connection between community and reaching out to our world in 1 John 1:3:

"We proclaim to you what we have seen and heard, so that you also may have fellowship with us. And our fellowship is with the Father and with his Son, Jesus Christ."

For many years, the church has taught an "individualistic invitational style" of evangelism: You, as an individual, go out and share your faith with another individual, and you invite that person to come into a "personal relationship with Jesus" (a phrase that isn't in the Bible).

The Bible teaches a community-based invitational style. A community of believers ("we") invite people into our fellowship (John's use of *our* fellowship is important; it indicates not just any kind of fellowship, but fellowship that was distinctly Christian)—a fellowship with the Father and his Son at its center.

> "Whoever would enter into the fellowship with the apostles would actually be entering into their fellowship with the Father and the Son."
>
> —*Life Application Bible Commentary*

The implications are:

➤ You, as a Christian, are in Christ-centered community.

➤ You invite others who are not in that community.

➤ When people come, they have the opportunity to join not only in your community, but, by it's essence, into communion with God.

Bridge-Building, Bridge-Crossing Groups

Christians have used the "bridge illustration" for years to share their faith. My niece Julie used it effectively to lead me to Jesus. It used to be that leaders would draw in community or small groups on the right side of the illustration, representing that once you have crossed the bridge you should get into fellowship with other Christians.

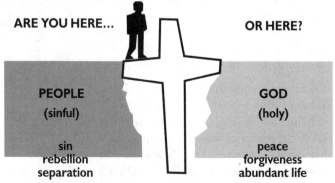

ARE YOU HERE...   **OR HERE?**

PEOPLE
(sinful)

sin
rebellion
separation

GOD
(holy)

peace
forgiveness
abundant life

That worked to a large extent years ago, when most Americans were relatively close to the gap. Christianity was still the dominant faith in the country, it had a relatively good reputation, and people were fairly accepting of it. It didn't take much to move people toward the bridge.

Today, however, the bridge is miles away from many Americans. It is obscured by negativity about Christianity and many other large cultural and societal barriers.

That's why the new science is to place small group community on the left side of the illustration. Your small groups can meet people where they are, serve them, and invite them into your community with a cause. Then you can walk with them together through the various pits and obstacles to the bridge.

Bill Hybels, senior minister at Willow Creek Community Church in South Barrington, Illinois, has said that believers have two gifts to give to the world. One is Jesus (John 3:16) and the other is our community.

The Profound Power of Community

The apostle John also wrote what I think is the most amazing passage about community in the Bible: John 17:20-26. This passage shows the profound power of authentic community.

➤ Jesus is praying for you and me here: "My prayer is not for them alone. I pray also for those who will believe in me through their message" (v. 20). He is praying for one simple and yet extraordinary thing, that we may be one…just as he and the Father are one! His deep desire for us is to experience the kind of community that the Godhead experiences.

➤ When we do relate to one another as Jesus and the Father relate—when we live in real, authentic community—we can have a huge impact on our world: "May they also be in us so that the world may believe that you have sent me" (v. 21). When we live in outward-focused community, the world will believe in Jesus.

A Community Strategy

Jesus has given us a strategy for reaching non-Christians in our world. It is repeated often throughout the gospels. It really is, by its nature, an excellent small group strategy. It's simply:

"One of the things that most impresses the world is the way Christians love each other and live together in harmony...The lost world cannot see God, but they can see Christians; and what they see in us is what they will believe about God. If they see love and unity, they will believe that God is love. If they see hatred and division, they will reject the message of the Gospel."[2]

—Warren Wiersbe

Come and see...Go and tell...
Come and see...Go and tell...

The abundant life is not just about coming to Jesus; it's also about going and telling others about him. Your small group is much more than just a "come and see" group; it's also a "go and tell" group. So go and tell what you've seen and heard...so that they can come into fellowship with you and see how good God really is!

How to Start Going and Telling

So, how do you get started becoming a "go and tell" group? It all starts with you, the leader.

1. *You must go first and model it for your group members.* If they don't see your compassion for lost friends—if you don't even have any lost friends!—it's unlikely they will get excited about going and telling as a group.

2. *Make going and telling a lifestyle.* Evangelism is not a program; it's what flows from the heart of a Christian who truly loves God and loves people. As Jim Petersen said in *Living Proof*, "This kind of evangelism can hardly be called an activity in which one engages on certain occasions. It is *life*. Living itself becomes evangelistic."[3]

3. *To do either of the first two, you must begin with prayer.*

- Pray that God will give you his heart for the lost sheep.

- Ask him for opportunities to go and tell.

- Ask him to open your eyes to the harvest.

- Begin praying for people in your circles of influence by name. Pray for their needs (you may need to ask). Ask God to draw them to himself.

The key factor is prayer. I came across the following quote on the Internet: "Evangelism without intercession is like an explosive without a detonator. Intercession without evangelism is like a detonator without an explosive."[4]

> " I pray that you may be active in sharing your faith, so that you will have a full understanding of every good thing we have in Christ. "
>
> —Philemon 6

God has given you the responsibility and opportunity—as his ambassador—to share what he has freely given you. And he will never leave you alone in the task.

Next, help the group begin going and telling. If this is new, take one level at a time.

THREE LEVELS OF GOING AND TELLING IN A SMALL GROUP

LEVEL 1: Support One Another's Efforts

TRY THIS!

I've used "The Blessing List," from TOUCH Outreach Ministries as a tool for systematic prayer for non-Christian friends. See www.touchusa.org

✳ Use icebreakers that get members talking about their non-Christian friends, neighbors, coworkers, and family members.

✳ Learn how to go and tell (*Go Fish, The Contagious Christian, Walk Across the Room, Living Proof*).

✳ Make applications of your current study to going and telling.

✳ Pray.

LEVEL 2: Go Together to Plant Seeds

* Throw a "Matthew Party." This is a party, based on Matthew 9:9-13, to which you invite a few members of your small group and their non-Christian friends. Nothing particularly "spiritual" has to be planned. Just pray first and watch for what God does.

* Leverage people in the group with evangelism gifts. Perhaps hand off ownership of this group role to them. Other group members might invite evangelism-gifted members to meet a non-Christian friend. (Some have the supernatural gift of evangelism, but we're all called to go and tell).

* Leverage church events strategically. As a group, discuss who you can invite. Pray together for the event beforehand.

* Leverage social events of members. To what events can group members invite their friends? Sports events? Art fairs? Car shows?

LEVEL 3: Invite Seekers to Your Group

* Use the "Empty Chair." Leave a chair open to symbolize the fact that you are open to new people joining you. Pray for the person(s) who will fill your empty chair.

* Use natural curriculum rhythms. Invite people to join you at the beginning of a new study so they are on the same page as the rest of the group. Purposely study a subject that non-Christian friends may be interested in considering (i.e. marriage, raising children, and finances).

* Remember, the leader must go first!

I'm A Leader... Now What? **73**

One of my favorite scenes is a small group who has helped a friend cross the bridge celebrating together as their friend is baptized. Sometimes it happens in a swimming pool or hot tub of a member's home. Sometimes it happens at the church building with one of the group members baptizing their friend.

Either way, it's a fulfillment of 1 John 1:3. The group has proclaimed to this person what they have seen and heard so that their friend could have real fellowship with them. Now, this new Christian has fellowship not only with them, but with the Father and his Son, Jesus Christ. That is a reason to celebrate!

MORE THAN YOU CAN IMAGINE!

What are your plans for your small group? From my experience, if they were honest, many small group leaders would say something like, "To get through my lesson this week." Some groups may have plans through the current study, but few that I've seen have a one- or two-year plan. That's unfortunate, because research shows that goal setting is one of the main factors in helping small groups grow and multiply themselves.

I want to close this chapter by encouraging you to plan. But don't just make a human-designed, human-sized plan; make a God-activated, God-sized plan for your group. A God-sized plan (GSP) should make you and you're group gasp, *No way we can do that!* (and that, of course, is the point). It should drive your group to your knees. It should be so big that if God isn't in it, it's destined to fail. In the corporate world, this is called a BHAG: a "Big Hairy Audacious Goal."

> "Put God in charge of your work, then what you've planned will take place." —Proverbs 16:3

> The BHAG concept comes from Jim Collins in his book *Good to Great*. See his web site at http://www. jimcollins.com.

The best small group leader ever made God-sized plans. He had a three-year plan for his group: To turn a bunch of uneducated, ordinary, smelly fishermen into fishers of men. To turn them into world changers. This was also a God-activated plan. Remember, Jesus did nothing except what the Father gave him to do.

Then he gave his followers a God-sized plan: to go and make disciples of all nations. *All* nations! That's God-sized!

How will you determine your GSP?
Do each of these yourself first, and then do each with your group.

1. Ask it. Begin by praying about it, asking God what his plan is, and taking time to really listen to him.

2. Imagine it. Ask yourself this question: What if God…? You fill in the blank. What is something so big that if God isn't in it, it's destined to fail?

3. Let God expand it. You've asked for and imagined something big, hopefully really big. Now read Ephesians 3:20: "With God's power working in us, God can do much, much more than anything we can ask or imagine" (*New Century Version*).

Once you know what it is, be sure to crystallize it. Write it down on paper, including all the steps and who will do what. (This is where group members with the spiritual gift of administration can help. Let them use their gifts!)

Your GSP will undoubtedly involve serving others in some way. But you as a leader have already started serving your group by including them in all the

Remember: Goal setting is one of the main factors in helping small groups grow and multiply themselves.

planning. That's great, because one of the best ways you can serve is to share leadership with others in the group. When you do, you'll impact your group, your church, and the world! More on that in Chapter 6.

NOW WHAT?

Take a first crack at writing a possible GSP for your group. This may not end up being the real thing, but you can get the process started in the space below.

---

[1] This list taken from the text of *Leadership By the Book* by Ken Blanchard, Bill Hybels, and Phil Hodges (New York: William Morrow & Company, 1999), 42, 43.

[2] Warren Wiersbe, *Bible Exposition Commentary—New Testament,* Volume I (ivictor.com, 2002, in WORDsearch, 2005), chapter 18.

[3] Jim Petersen, *Living Proof,* fourth printing (Colorado Springs: NavPress, 1991), 120.

4 Quoted on an e-mail listserv from evangelist Reinhard Bonnke.

5 This list is a collection of material I've pulled together from various sources. The framework and some of the contents came from a Willow Creek Small Groups Conference.

Share

Sharing is a fundamental concept. Most of us learned how to do it in Kindergarten. So why do so many people still struggle with it?

Sharing is also an elementary aspect of small group life. I've been alluding to it throughout this book. The fact is, if you've *surrendered* "your" leadership to God, you'll find it natural to share leadership with others. If you are *shepherding* group members toward spiritual growth, you'll realize that as you guide them toward Christlikeness, you are moving them onward to servant-leadership. And as I mentioned in the last chapter, if you are truly *serving* the group, you will let them do some of the leading.

> **Share:**
> 1: *have in common;* 2: *use jointly or in common* 3: *have, give, or receive a share of, [syn: partake, partake in]* 4: *give out as one's portion or share* (WordNet® 2.0).

Learning to share happens in three stages: promoting partnership, building teamwork, and breeding leadership.

PROMOTE PARTNERSHIP

On a group mountain bike ride, we were rolling alongside a creek when my front tire hit a deep rut, throwing me off. My bike fell about eight feet toward the creek. I went down after it, of course, but then could get neither myself nor my bike up the creek's steep, muddy embankment. Fortunately, my friend David was right there to pull me up. It reminded me of a favorite Bible verse:

Two are better than one,
because they have a good return for their work:

> If one falls down,
> his friend can help him up.
> But pity the man who falls
> and has no one to help him up!
>
> —Ecclesiastes 4:9, 10

Promote partnership within your small group.

I've learned a lot about the Christian life on my bicycles. I used to ride alone on both my road and mountain bikes, but I've learned that group rides are best! I like having others there to pick me up. We encourage one another and push each other to go farther, faster, and more dangerously! I love the return for our work when several of us on our road bikes take turns at the front as the others draft and get a little break.

Two are better than one on the road, on the trail, and all along the journey. I see the same principles at work in healthy small groups.

- **When groups really do ride through life together—not just attend meetings together—life really is better. God created us to live life in partnership with others.**

- **We need each other to "pick us up." In group life we need to become less independent, yet not unhealthily dependent on each other. The aim is a healthy interdependence—partnership.**

- **When individuals take turns at the front and everyone plays a part in the group's work, there is a tremendous, synergistic return for the work.**

- **We should have pity—compassion— for the person who does not have this kind of community.**

The next step in learning to share is to build teamwork.

Definitions

Synergy: The interaction of two or more agents or forces so that their combined effect is greater than the sum of their individual effects (*American Heritage Dictionary*).

BUILD TEAMWORK

I have a confession. I like Mike. I like Mike so much I named my first son after him—well, kind of. My son's name is Jordan Michael. I like Mike so much I was selected as the biggest Michael Jordan fan in Anderson, Indiana, in 1993 (the year of M.J.'s first retirement). I like Michael Jordan for a reason: I like basketball and he is the greatest basketball player of all time.[1] And yet his first NBA team, the Chicago Bulls, did not win the NBA championship until his seventh season. That's when they assembled a great team around the greatest player.

Everyone Brings Something to the Group

Small groups are much like sports teams. One player, or one leader, does not make a winning team. It takes participation by everyone—teamwork.

That's the essence of the apostle Paul's description in 1 Corinthians 12 of the church as a body. What goes for the church as a whole also goes for small groups. Although one person may lead as the group's shepherd, each person has a gift to share with the rest of the group. Some may lead in hospitality, others may lead in administration or serving or encouraging or contributing to others' needs or showing mercy.

> "The body is not made up of one part but of many."
> —1 Corinthians 12:14

There are basically three ways to determine people's gifts, abilities, and interests:

❶ The first is to use a gifts assessment tool. These can be valuable, but they're not relational and I believe they can pigeon-hole people. I believe there are better, more organic ways of discovering gifts in a small group.

❷ Another way is simply to ask, "What do you enjoy doing? How can you help lead this group? What have you found you're gifted at? What do other people say you're good at?"

❸ Another way to discover gifts is to watch. As the group gets to know one another, people's gifts will start to become obvious—usually to everyone but themselves! Take time at

**a meeting to affirm each other's gifts. The group tells each
person, in turn, what his or her gift is and why each person
is an essential part of the team.**

As people's gifts become obvious, find ways to utilize them. People can play
numerous roles—everything from timekeeper and tension reliever to social planner, service coordinator, and prayer leader.

Teamwork Drills

I love coaching kids sports teams, especially basketball. One of the most
rewarding parts of coaching for me is taking a rag-tag group of kids who don't
know one another at the beginning of a season and turning them into a *team*. A
team works together as one; each using his unique abilities for the good of the
whole. A team wins because five are better than one. It takes a lot of effort to
build this teamwork—lots of drills and time spent together, both in and outside
of practices and games.

Building a productive team as
a small group is much the same. It
takes intentional effort, both inside
and outside group meeting times.
It takes team-building drills such as
these:

➤ Go on a camping or
   hiking trip together and
   give each person a
   specific assignment.

➤ Play a game such a
   volleyball, paintball,
   or a role-playing game
   against another group.

**"It takes 10 hands to
score a basket."**

—Coach John Wooden

➤ Participate in a shared work experience or serving
   opportunity.

➤ Identify a common "enemy" or challenge together.

Remove the Obstacles to Teamwork

The biggest obstacle to building a team is a leader who will not or cannot share. I've found there are three main obstacles:

1. The Heart: Some leaders have difficulty handing off responsibilities to others. It's either a lack of trust or a need to control, but either way, this attitude asphyxiates the group.

2. The Habits: Some leaders have simply not learned to share leadership. When they were asked to lead they thought it was their job to do everything, so they do. They lead by habit.

3. The Head: I've known some leaders who are really good at everything—except building a team. Even though they have exceptional facilitation skills and Bible knowledge, their groups are unhealthy, stagnant, and sometimes struggling to survive. Why? Because group members do not sense they are really needed. The leader does everything. The rest of the group just attends the meetings. They learn a lot from the studies and like other members of the group, and if that is enough to satisfy them they'll stick around, but not much more.

If you have trouble building a team, what is your obstacle?

If it's the *heart,* ask God to help you change your attitude; ask for humility. As I mentioned in

> In Chapter 4 (in the "Guide Them to Authenticity" section), I showed you how to start your group as a team. Refer back to that section if you're just getting started. In this chapter, I'm assuming you've built your group as a team. Now it's time to work together more productively as a

CHECK THIS OUT!

There are lots of good books about building teams. My favorite three are:

- *The One Minute Manager Builds High Performing Teams*, Ken Blanchard, Donald Carew, and Eunice Parisi-Carew, William Morrow and Company
- *Doing Church as a Team*, Wayne Cordeiro, Regal
- *Wooden on Leadership*, John Wooden, McGraw Hill

Chapter 3, humility precedes surrender. It's not too difficult for a humble leader to surrender control of the group. Begin by asking God to change your heart to be more like Jesus'.

If it is the *habits:*

1. learn the skills of building a highly functioning team

2. change your habit

3. let your group know things are going to be different

4. apologize for not giving them opportunities and responsibilities in the past

5. ask them to remind you to let them be involved

If it is the *head*, you probably need to recognize the issue and simply back off from doing everything. Swallow your pride; other group members may not lead the same way as you. Another attitude you may need to deal with is *perfectionism*. If that's you, work at becoming perfect at letting others be involved, even if they're not as good as you!

With God's help you can turn around the situations by removing the obstacles that keep you from building a team. One of the qualities of a great team is that everyone is working together toward a common goal. As a team, be sure to identify your goals— your God-sized plans—together, and then, as a team, *just do it!*

Breed Leadership

Joe and Marlene are a happily married couple with kids. Joe works on the loading dock of a trucking company and Marlene works at a fast-food restaurant. Their three children, Hank, Susan, and Kenneth are very bright. The whole family loves Jesus, and each week they faithfully go to church. They have family devotions together after dinner each evening, and the children don't just sit there and endure it—they look forward to it and participate. Joe and Marlene are proud parents and love their family!

> "We're going to turn this team around 360 degrees."
> — Jason Kidd upon being drafted to the Dallas Mavericks

Hank, the oldest, enjoys writing science fiction stories and shares a bedroom with his brother, Kenny. Susan has always been helpful around the house and cares for the family dog. Kenny, while not nearly as studious as Hank or Susan, is a good athlete and enjoys playing basketball and soccer.

> **"Point your kids in the right direction—when they're old they won't be lost."**
> —Proverbs 22:6, *The Message*

What observations would you make about this family? Would you say they are healthy and on the right track? As Paul Harvey would say, "Now the rest of the story":

Joe and Marlene have been married 46 years. Joe is 67 and Marlene will be 63 this year. Hank is 43, Susan is 37, and Kenny, the youngest, was a bit of a surprise to Joe and Marlene. He's 29 years old. All three graduated from college.[2]

Now that you know this additional information, what do you think of this family? What do you think needs to change in this home? Why?

One more question: On a scale of one to five, how similar is your small group to this fictional family?

Avoid Extinction—Guide Group Members to Continued Growth

Small groups are best described as spiritual families. An essential value is that family members grow up and leave home! A family in which the kids never leave home would be considered unhealthy and unnatural.

> **"Make sure you tell your children, and your children tell their children, And their children their children. Don't let this message die out."**
> —Joel 1:3, *The Message*

The same is true of small groups! Producing and sending out new leaders is a natural occurrence in a healthy group. As the group leader— a spiritual parent—you help guide this family to maturity. Newer Christians still need to be on "pure spiritual milk" (1 Peter 2:2). They need to learn the basics of Christianity, led by more mature members of the group. As believ-

I'm A Leader... Now What? **83**

ers mature, they become ready to eat solid food (1 Corinthians 3:2). As they continue to grow in their faith, they are given opportunities to lead others and eventually to step out to lead their own spiritual family.

This is called *multiplication*. Multiplication is a natural, fundamental principle of life. Throughout Genesis, God says, "Be fruitful and increase in numbers (multiply)." Jesus' marching orders for his church involves multiplication. What happens to a family or any other organization that does not multiply itself? Like Joe and Marlene's family, first it become very dysfunctional and then unhealthy. Eventually it becomes extinct!

As people in your group are growing in their faith, the natural next step is for you to help them step out and lead others. Why? I can think of at least two reasons, one biblical and one developmental:

> **Community is like a ship; everyone ought to be prepared to take the helm.**
>
> **—Henrik Ibsen**

1. **The Bible describes a process of spiritual growth that results in leading others. Hebrews 5:11–6:1 assumes that as you are becoming a mature follower of Jesus, that you step out to lead others.**

2. **The best way for your group members to continue growing is for them to step out of their comfort zones and begin leading others. A new Christian grows rapidly. After awhile, however, that growth begins to slow down and eventually becomes incremental at best. Individuals can remain in this plateaued state for years attending small group faithfully every week and yet not growing. To begin to grow spiritually again, they need a challenge that will spur on their growth and make them rely more on God's power. People who have stepped out on faith discover that they grow more than ever. The best thing you can do for plateaued group members is to move them out of your group!**

> ### Word to the Wise
>
> "There is so much more we would like to say about this. But you don't seem to listen, so it's hard to make you understand. You have been Christians a long time now, and you ought to be teaching others. Instead, you need someone to teach you again the basic things a beginner must learn about the Scriptures.... Let us go on instead and become mature."
>
> —Hebrews 5:11–6: 1, *NLT*

Small groups have accurately been described as "leader breeders." When you emphasize helping people grow spiritually, new leaders naturally rise up. As they participate in team leadership, they will be prepared to lead. If you've done everything else in this book, you won't be able to hold them back!

How to Develop and Deploy Leaders

The best small group leader ever was, once again, the perfect example for us. He modeled developing and deploying his group members. In his group, every one of the members—with the possible exception of one—was a leader in training.

> "You will either step forward into growth or you will step back into safety."
> —Abraham Maslow

Jesus began with a goal for their development from the beginning: to make them into church leaders—"fishers of men." He told them the plan and then executed it. He spent time with them over three years, modeling everything he wanted them to learn. Over time they became a team. He gave them opportunities to lead along the way, allowing them to make mistakes. Each time they were involved in servant leadership, he would meet with them afterwards and debrief. He would use those opportunities to teach them valuable lessons on leadership. Finally he sent them out with a mission. As they stepped out to lead, he stayed available for them when they needed him. He promised he would never leave them.

> "Long before modern managers, Jesus was busy preparing people for the future. He wasn't aiming to pick a crown prince, but a successor generation. When the time came for Him to leave, He did not put in place a crash program of leadership development—the curriculum had been taught for three years in a living classroom."
>
> —Leighton Ford, *Transforming Leadership*

Jesus provided guidelines for you as you discover, develop, and deploy leaders:

1. From the very beginning, have a plan for their development. Have a clear picture in your mind of what you hope they will become.

2. Tell them the plan. Let them know up-front that they will be sent out to do the same with others. Repeat this step regularly!

3. Consider *everyone* a potential leader-in-training. When you look at their hearts, perhaps some don't look much like leaders yet. Your responsibility is to shepherd and develop them so they do.

4. Spend time with them. There's no substitute for time in community.

5. Build a team with them. Share leadership roles.

6. Give them opportunities to lead parts of the meeting and carry out other group leadership responsibilities.

7. Increase leadership opportunities over time. Allow them to make mistakes.

8. Always debrief a leadership experience. Provide positive feedback and helpful critiques.

9. As you work as a team together, watch for teachable moments. Use these to help them grow in servant-leadership.

10. Send them out. Continue to be available to them as they need help—more involved at first, backing off over time.

Pass the Baton

At our church I give batons, the ones used in relay races, to new leaders. The batons have the phrase, "Pass it on" etched upon them.

"It may take only a moment to pass a baton, but it takes much longer to pass the heart of the baton."[3]

—Wayne Cordeiro

Three of my kids run track, so I've watched a lot of relays. I've noticed several things about these races that I think are applicable to small group leadership:

❶ Everyone on the relay team participates.

❷ The team spends a lot of time preparing for their handoffs. They have a strategy for how it will happen. A good, clean handoff is vital.

❸ The runner receiving the baton begins running before the preceding runner gets to him. He expects the baton; it's not a surprise. He builds up speed and waits for the handoff.

❹ The one holding the baton is responsible for making a clean handoff to the next runner.

In small groups, you pass the baton not because you are finished with the race but to include others in on the race! Don't wait to pass your baton when you are concluding your group. Pass it on as soon as someone has said yes to being a leader-in-training. Let them run for awhile with it and then pass it to someone else. Pass out lots of batons! Yours is a different kind of relay team—a team that passes out batons liberally, because the need for more leaders is great!

The Need is Great

Earlier I discussed the visionary passage in Matthew 9:35-38. Let's look at it again from a different perspective. Jesus' compassion for the crowds led him to do something. He didn't just size up the situation, say, "Wow, that's a shame," and keep going. His compassion moved him to action. But not the kind of action many people would take. Jesus' approach was not, *Get 'er done.* It was, *Get prayin'!*

The first thing Jesus did was the first thing he always did: he surrendered it to the Father. He told his disciples, "The harvest is so great, but the workers are so few. So pray to the Lord who is in charge of the harvest to send out more workers."

The harvest is still great. And the workers are still few.

I believe many of the workers will be people just like you—not "professionals," but ordinary people who are already in the harvest fields—in their neighborhoods, workplaces, schools, and families. At the ballparks, gyms, coffee shops, and a variety of other places in the world. They are people who could make a tremendous impact on the world by shepherding ten to twelve people or so in a small group, and not just any group, but a group with God-sized plans.

NOW WHAT?

➤ To whom in your group are you going to pass the baton? Write their names here.

➤ What's your plan for building more teamwork and multiplying your leadership? Take some time and write it down on a separate sheet of paper.

[1] Michael Jordan led the NBA in scoring ten times (an NBA record), including seven straight times from 1987-1993. He has the highest career points per game average, holds the record for most seasons leading the league in scoring-10, shares the record for the most consecutive seasons leading the league in scoring—7, and had a streak of nine consecutive games scoring 40 points or more. He was the Most Valuable Player five times, Defensive Player of the Year (1988), steals leader three times, nine-time All-Defensive First Team (1988-93, 1996-98), Rookie of the Year (1985), fourteen-time all-star, All-Star MVP three times, all-time scoring leader in All-Star history, won tile All-Star Slam Dunk Contest two times, and two-time Olympic gold medallist.

[2] This story is excerpted from my self-published booklet, *Leaving Home*.

[3] Wayne Cordeiro, *Doing Church as a Team* (Ventura, California: Regal, 2001), 114. Cordeiro is senior pastor at New Hope Christian Fellowship in Honolulu, Hawaii.

Steward

I spent time today, on a break from writing, back in my woods. I call them mine, even though they belong to our neighborhood association, because of the amount of time I've spent working back there. I've blazed a mountain-bike trail through the woods, complete with log jumps, creek crossings, ramps, and other adventures. I routinely maintain the trail and the woods, cleaning up garbage, removing log jams in the creek, and sawing and removing downed trees that block the path.

Steward:
Someone who manages property or other affairs for someone else. (WordNet® 2.0).

These woods are not only my refuge, they're my little piece of creation that I get to work. They are my garden of Eden. I identify with Adam when I'm in my woods. He was given a place like this to enjoy and manage (Genesis 1:26). It was an act of stewardship.

I've thought about this as I've worked in my woods. God created it all and controls it all. But part of his design was to give us stewardship over what is his—to manage it and work alongside him in caring for it. Sometimes as I remove some sticks that are impeding the flow of the creek, I can immediately see a difference in the direction of the water. This might sound silly, but I seek to be in tune with God enough to sense how I can best work together with him to tend to these woods. After all, they don't belong to me or the neighborhood association. They're God's, but I am his partner.

> "Let us make human beings in our image, make them reflecting our nature so they can be responsible for the fish in the sea, the birds in the air, the cattle, and, yes, Earth itself, and every animal that moves on the face of Earth."
>
> —Genesis 1:26, *The Message*

THE STEWARDSHIP MODEL

Jesus was the perfect example of a good steward. It is obvious in the Gospels that he lived his life on earth as a steward of all God gave him. Of particular interest is how he illustrated stewardship of the small group entrusted to his care. Seven times in John 17:6-19, Jesus referred to the disciples as being his, given to him by the Father while he was here on earth. He discussed what he came to do: to pass on to them what the Father had given him (vv. 8, 13, 14). He talked about multiplication—that he was leaving them behind and that he was sending them into the world just as he had been sent (vv. 11, 18).

Jesus' attitude about his small group is reflected in his summation: "None has been lost except the one doomed to destruction" (v. 12). Not only had they not been lost, but they *won* thousands to Christ just a few weeks later and started a movement that changed the world. That never would have happened if it had not been for Jesus' attitude of stewardship as he surrendered his will to God's eternal purpose (see Ephesians 3:11).

> ## THE BEST SMALL GROUP LEADER EVER SAID...
>
> "I have told these men about you. They were in the world, but then you gave them to me. Actually, they were always yours, and you gave them to me; and they have kept your word. Now they know that everything I have is a gift from you."
>
> —John 17:6, 7, *NLT*

Remember:
God has an eternal purpose for your small group, too. It will be accomplished when you surrender to it as an act of stewardship.

THE STEWARDSHIP GUIDE

Jesus modeled stewardship for us, and he also spent a lot of time speaking about it. We generally apply Jesus' teachings on stewardship to money, but that's just a small part of the picture. God wants you to wisely manage everything he gives you.

In the parable of the talents in Matthew 25:14-30, Jesus gives a number of guidelines for how you can lead your group as an act of stewardship.

I. The Group Is God's, Not Yours

"A man going on a journey...called his servants and entrusted his property to them" (Matthew 25:14).

You have been called to lead something that does not belong to you. It belongs to the Master who has entrusted you, the servant, with the responsibility to invest into your group members while they are in your care.

As the group shepherd, you have been given a huge trust, responsibility, and privilege. As our main passage puts it: "Be shepherds of God's flock that is under your care" (1 Peter 5:2). As a small group leader, God has entrusted you with much! He's entrusted you with his people, his message, and his mission!

I've discussed being a steward of his people and his mission, but what about his *message?* The apostle Paul sent this warning to the Galatian leaders: "Let me be blunt: If one of us—even if an angel from heaven!—were to preach something other than what we preached originally, let him be cursed" (Galatians 1:8, *The Message*).

This statement is so important, Paul repeated it a second time: "I said it once; I'll say it again: If anyone, regardless of reputation or credentials, preaches something other than what you received originally, let him be cursed" (v. 9).

The reason Scripture cautions us about sound teaching is obvious. We are handling the truth. Anyone who leads or teaches any kind of group has a high privilege and responsibility. This does not mean, however, that leaders and teachers must be exceptionally talented, highly educated individuals. The apostles were known as "unschooled, ordinary men" (Acts 4:13).

As you lead, you are responsible not only for the group God has given you and his mission, but to correctly handle the word of truth (2 Timothy 2:15).

> ### Caution
>
> The theme of stewarding God's message is repeated elsewhere in Scripture:
>
> - "Not many of you should presume to be teachers, my brothers, because you know that we who teach will be judged more strictly" (James 3:1).
>
> - "Let the word of Christ dwell in you richly as you teach and admonish one another *with all wisdom*" (Colossians 3:16, *my emphasis*).
>
> - "You must teach what is *in accord with sound doctrine*" (Titus 2:1, *my emphasis*).

2. God Gives in Different Proportions

"To one he gave five talents of money, to another two talents, and to another one talent, each according to his ability" (Matthew 25:15).

It's interesting that the Master gives different amounts to the different servants. At first that doesn't seem fair. But the Master only gave what each servant was *capable of handling* ("according to his ability"). Think about it this way: Why would God give you more than you can handle? He promises never to give you beyond what you can bear (1 Corinthians 10:13). That's better than fair. That's his grace at work!

God already knows the capacity of our hearts. So he gives generously to the one with the big heart, because he knows that this servant is most capable, spiritually, to bring a bigger return. But he gives the poor steward the minimum amount because he is not as capable to handle the larger responsibility; his heart capacity is smaller.

Each one of the servants acted in accordance with the capacity of his heart. If you want God to entrust you with more—more group members, more influence, more friends, etc.—increase your heart capacity in that area! That begins with what you learned in Chapters 2 and 3—seeking and surrendering to him!

3. God Settles Accounts

"After a long time the master of those servants returned and settled accounts with them" (Matthew 25:19).

> "Yes, each of us will have to give a personal account to God."
> —Romans 14:12, *NLT*

The events in this parable will actually happen some day. You and I will stand before the Master and we will account for how we handled what God blessed us with (see Matthew 12:36; 2 Corinthians 5:10; and Hebrews 4:13). God expects a good ROI (Return On his Investment). He expects more than what he left us with.

When you stand before the Master, what do you think he will ask you? I don't know for sure, but if he asks about the group he entrusted you with, it may be questions like these:

* **Did it grow?**
* **Are members more spiritually mature than when you started ?**
* **Are they living more abundantly?**
* **How did you invest your life into theirs and how did you invest them into the lives of others?**
* **Did you share leadership of the group with them?**
* **Did any of them step up to become leaders?**
* **Did you multiply the ministry of your group or bury in the ground what God entrusted to you?**

My hope and prayer for you is that someday, when you stand before the Master, ready to receive that crown of glory that will never fade away, that his response to you will be, "Well done, good and faithful servant! Well done!"

4. God Judges You on Your Faithfulness

"Well done, good and faithful servant! You have been faithful with a few things; I will put you in charge of many things" (Matthew 25:21).

God will not judge you on what you have done or not done. He will not judge you on your abilities or skills. He'll judge you someday on your faithfulness to him, on your stewardship.

That means he will also judge you on your lack of faithfulness. I think it's fascinating that the poor steward said, "I was afraid, so I hid…" (v. 25). Sound familiar? Adam said the same words in the Garden of Eden when he sinned (Genesis 3:10). That too was a sin of poor stewardship. God had entrusted the Garden to Adam's care and cultivation with only one condition. Adam decided to do things his way rather than God's way. The result of this lack of faithfulness—this poor stewardship, this sin—is fear and inauthenticity. We've been hiding ever since.

5. God Gives and Takes Away!

"For everyone who has will be given more, and he will have an abundance. Whoever does not have, even what he has will be taken from him" (Matthew 25:28).

God gave Adam and Eve the Garden and God took it away from them when they were not good stewards of it. The Master gave the last servant something to invest and God took it away when the man buried it in the ground.

> "The Lord God placed the man in the Garden of Eden to tend and care for it. But the Lord God gave him this warning: 'You may freely eat any fruit in the garden except fruit from the tree of the knowledge of good and evil.'"
> —Genesis 2:15-17, *NLT*

God has given you a group of people to invest into. He will either give you more, if you are good and faithful in your stewardship, or he will take it away if you aren't. If he takes it away, he will give those group members to a good and faithful group leader. I see this happen in the church all the time. One group leader complains, either because he started with only a few people or because no one stays. Another leader doesn't know what to do with all the people God keeps sending. She starts with a good-sized group and then even more come. She subgroups so everyone can be involved and shares leadership with everyone in the group, and they keep coming!

The group doesn't close its doors—that would be like burying what God has given them! People keep growing and the more they grow the more people they bring. They serve as a team together, which increases the capacity of their hearts even more. They go and tell people who are lost, like sheep without a shepherd, and they come too! People are leaving other groups to come to this one.

God is giving to them abundantly—more than they can even ask or imagine! The group members, as well as the houses where they meet, are overflowing! They keep investing and inviting, inviting and investing. They multiply the group not once, not three times, but, eventually, a hundred times over!

THE BEST SMALL GROUP LEADER EVER SAID...

"From everyone who has been given much, much will be demanded; and from the one who has been entrusted with much, much more will be asked."
—Luke 12:48

What's the difference between these two groups? The capacity of the leaders' hearts, which can be measured by six vital heart attributes:

- **Seek**
- **Surrender**
- **Shepherd**
- **Serve**
- **Share**
- **Steward**

These were the attributes of the Master's heart as well.

NOW WHAT?

➤ Measure the capacity of your heart using the following scales. Be honest!

1 = a tiny heart, like the worthless servant
5 = a big heart, like the best small group leader ever

Seek	1	2	3	4	5
Surrender	1	2	3	4	5
Shepherd	1	2	3	4	5
Serve	1	2	3	4	5
Share	1	2	3	4	5
Steward	1	2	3	4	5

➤ How are these interrelated?

➤ Where do you need to grow most right now?

➤ What's your first step?

CHECK OUT THIS VAUABLE COUPON!

FREE

SMALL GROUP RESOURCES

For MORE HELP, check out the small group leader resources on *SmallGroups.com*.

With the purchase of this book, you are entitled to a free one-month membership at *www.SmallGroups.com*. To claim your **FREE** membership:

> ➤ Go to: *www.SmallGroups.com/freemembership.*
> ➤ Continue through "checkout" process.
> ➤ Select payment method "check/money order." However, no payment is due if you use coupon code: **stdsg06**
> ➤ Then click "Redeem" and "Confirm Order" for your free membership!

Redeem your coupon *today!*